Cross-Border Taxes

A guide for Americans living in Canada

Cori Carl

Contents

Introduction	11
Do I need to file taxes in Canada?	14
What if I lived outside of Canada this year?	14
Short stays in Canada	14
Do I need to file taxes in the US?	15
What happens if I haven't filed US taxes?	15
How much of this do I need to know	16
Do I need an accountant?	16
Which country do I pay taxes in?	16
Will I pay twice as much in tax?	17
Are taxes higher in Canada?	17
Understanding tax residency	17
Make sure you're no longer a US state resident	18
How much time can I spend out of the country and still be a Canadian resident?	18
Power of attorney and living wills	21
Tax filing deadlines	26
US tax deadlines	26
Canadian tax deadlines	26
Converting currency	26
Keeping track of expenses and deductions	27
Missing documents	27
US federal taxes	28
Your spouse	28
Treating your spouse as a resident alien	28
Treating your spouse as a non-resident alien	28
Gifts to your spouse	28
Attribution rules	29

Your salary...	29
Short stays in Canada	29
Foreign earned income exclusion	30
Foreign housing exclusion	32
State income	32
Your freelance and hobby income........................	33
Your business income...................................	33
Canadian companies	34
LLCs	34
Your home and cottage.................................	34
Home buyer tax credits	34
Mortgage interest deduction	35
Capital gains taxes on your home	35
Renting out part of your home	37
Your old home in the US	37
Gifting your home	38
Cross border trusts	38
Your investment property..............................	38
Deferring taxation	38
Capital gains taxes on investment properties	39
Your disability income.................................	39
Government retirement plans...........................	39
Your tax-sheltered accounts............................	41
401k & 403b	41
Your stocks, bonds, and mutual funds..................	46
Canadian mutual funds	46
Qualified small business shares	47
Canadian holding companies	47
Your inheritance.....................................	48
Other types of income................................	48

Taxes based on adjusted gross income	48
Net Investment Income Tax	48
Foreign tax credits and deductions	48
Your estate	48
Your executor	49
Your spouse	49
Your heirs	50
Avoiding probate	50
Planned giving	51
Your will	51
Setting up a trust	51
Living outside of Canada and the US	52
Canadian exit tax	52
Who does the exit tax apply to?	53
What gets taxed?	54
Are you really paying extra taxes?	54
Declaring yourself a non-resident	55
Reporting requirements as a non-resident	56
Returning to Canada after the exit tax	57
Relinquishing your US green card	57
Renouncing US citizenship	57
Expatriating acts	58
Expatriation taxes and fees	58
Filing Canadian taxes for the first time	61
Things to do when you first arrive in Canada	62
Personal details	62
A simple income tax return	64
A complex income tax return	64
Reporting your income	64
Tax credits	69

Common deductions	70
Foreign assets and income	72
After you file	73
Making a payment	73
Filing for a refund	73
CRA audits	73
Getting caught up	77
Filing US tax forms for previous years	77
Penalties for overdue taxes	78
Tax penalty abatement	78
Offers in compromise	78
Setting up a tax debt payment plan	78
Currently not collectible debts	79
Statute of limitations on collecting tax debt	79
The Simple 1040 scenario	80
More complex 1040 scenarios	80
Owing taxes	83
Tax refunds	84
RRSPs	84
TFSA, RESP & RDSPs	84
Canadian mutual funds	85
Other tax-treaty items	85
FBAR	85
FATCA	86
IRS audits	87
How IRS audits work	87
Canadian and US tax forms	92
Key differences in Canadian & US federal income tax systems	93
US state tax filing	95
Canadian and US business deductions	99

Sample TFSA / RESP / RDSP letter to the IRS.................. 102
Sample penalty abatement request letter 103
About the author.. 105

Copyright © 2019 by Cori Carl
Cover art by Cori Carl

welcomehomeontario.ca

All rights reserved.
This book, or parts thereof, may not be reproduced in any form without permission.

ISBN-13: 978-1678560003
ISBN-10: 1678560006
ASIN: B082YG5XW8

Introduction

Perhaps you picked up this book because you're wondering how an American can afford to live in Canada, short of committing tax fraud, if both countries tax our worldwide income.

The answer is simple: tax treaties.

If only it were so simple to carry out! You'll need to file taxes in both countries, even if you'll almost certainly only owe taxes in one. Filing taxes in Canada for the first time can be a little tricky, but it's much simpler than what you're used to from the US.

So many articles I come across refer to punishing tax reporting requirements, but you probably only have to file two papers with the Internal Revenue Service (IRS): the 1040 and the FBAR. Don't get scared into shelling out thousands of dollars to tax advisors each year for something you can do in less than an hour.

If you've filed your own taxes in the US, you can handle this on your own, too. The real work of filing your taxes is the tedium of gathering the information required, not actually filling out the forms.

Most of the issues that come up for US citizens living in Canada are champagne problems. If someone is paying taxes in both countries either they are in the 1% or they're doing something terribly wrong.

This is not meant to be a comprehensive tax guide for either country, although I cover everything the average filer will need to know. I focus on how the tax code differs between the two countries. These are the things you need to know if you're obligated to file taxes in both, both to file your taxes this year and to plan for your financial future.

Even the most comprehensive book can only provide general information and tax regulations change regularly. If you want personal tax advice, you should consult an accountant or financial planner.

Remember, you should always verify the advice you get from your financial planner, just as you should verify the information in this book. Tax preparers and software aim to ensure that the tax information you file is complete and doesn't contain mistakes, but it's still important to understand the big picture.

In case this isn't already clear, I'm not an accountant or an attorney. This is a starting point for your own research and/or a discussion with your trusted advisors, not financial or legal advice. However, I have had the fortune of being audited by both the IRS and the CRA, which felt like a pretty thorough fact-checking of the information contained in this guide. While I haven't made life choices specifically to make my tax reporting obligations as complicated as possible, looking at my taxes might give you that impression.

Part One: Understanding cross-border taxes

Plenty of people don't think they need to file taxes if they know they won't owe money to the Canada Revenue Agency (CRA) or Internal Revenue Service (IRS).

In the US you can live for many years and never file taxes. As long as the IRS doesn't receive information suggesting you have significant untaxed income, they'll probably let you be. Why? Because you probably qualify for a refund! Most people have taxes automatically deducted from their paycheques, so they've already paid into the system.

That's not how the CRA operates. If you don't file your taxes, the CRA will contact you to let you know they haven't received them and remind you to submit them. If you continue to ignore the CRA, they can freeze your Canadian bank accounts. This can happen even if you don't owe any tax money.

Do I need to file taxes in Canada?

Anyone staying in Canada for more than 183 days in a year can be considered a tax resident and needs to file taxes reporting their worldwide income to the CRA.

Even if you have no income, you should file your Canadian taxes. You'll likely qualify for refundable tax credits and it's a simple process.

If you have a low enough income that you're not required to file taxes (about $12k), you'll still want to establish your RRSP deduction limit and establish the guaranteed income supplement or working income tax benefit. This is especially important for young adults, even if they have low or no income.

What if I lived outside of Canada this year?

You probably have to file taxes in Canada, even if you lived outside of the country for the entire year. Even if you've been gone for several years, you can still be deemed a factual resident of Canada if you retain significant ties to Canada and intend to return.

This is an area of taxation that's widely misunderstood. Tax nerds will happily brag about how Canada's taxation system is based on residency, while US taxes are based on citizenship. That's technically true, but in order to stop being a Canadian resident for tax purposes you need to permanently sever your ties to Canada. While this is not the same as having to renounce your US citizenship to end your US tax obligations, it's pretty close.

This means that as a US citizen who has ties to Canada, you may be required to file taxes in three countries if you are living outside the US and Canada. You can't just move and stop filing with the CRA

If you are leaving Canada for good, you may have to deal with the exit tax. Don't worry, it's not nearly as ominous as it sounds and you probably don't have to pay anything. You will still need to file some paperwork, even if you don't owe taxes.

Short stays in Canada

If you're working in Canada, but you're not a tax resident, you may not need to file. This usually happens when your US employer sent you to Canada. They may have withheld payroll taxes and submitted them to the IRS or the CRA. If they paid the CRA, you might be due a tax refund.

You might qualify for a refund from the CRA if you made less than C$10k from Canadian sources during the year or if you were in Canada for less than 183 days in any 12 month period and your company isn't permanently based in Canada.

	Tax exempt employee	Taxable employee
Taxes paid to the CRA	File a tax return and a receive refund	File a tax return and pay tax or receive a refund
Taxes not paid to the CRA	No need to file in Canada	File a tax return and pay tax

This is an unusual situation. If any of this applies to you, your company HR department should be able to tell you how you need to file.

Do I need to file taxes in the US?

Living outside of the US doesn't mean you don't have to pay taxes. Having US citizenship or permanent resident status makes you a tax resident as far as the IRS is concerned. This means you will have to file taxes and report your worldwide income, even if you never step onto US soil.

There's one exception. If you earn less than $20k a year, you may not have to file a US tax return.

What happens if I haven't filed US taxes?

If you haven't filed your US taxes in previous years, you may have trouble the next time you try to enter the country. Theoretically, you could face being arrested or having your bank accounts frozen for owing money to the IRS.

However, that's exceedingly unlikely to happen to you. The US recognizes that nearly everyone living in Canada who has failed to file their US tax return would not owe money, given the foreign earned income exclusion (FEIE) and the tax treaty.

I'll discuss how to file your back taxes for the US and what penalties you might face.

The CRA and IRS exchange information. In 2018 I amended my US return and decided to wait for the IRS to accept the changes before amending my Canadian return. I heard from the CRA about it before I heard back from the IRS!

If you make a large amount of money in Canada and don't report it in the US, the IRS can see the money in your Canadian accounts. They will not be happy.

If you're a Canadian citizen, the CRA will not assist the IRS in collecting any money you may owe. The Canadian court system won't enforce judgements for taxes you owe in the US. In this case, the IRS can only seize your US assets. This still seems like a terrible situation to be in.

If you aren't a Canadian citizen, the CRA may assist the IRS in collecting US tax debt.

How much of this do I need to know

You'll want to know this, even if you have an accountant.

Don't simply hand a stack of paperwork to your accountant and hope for the best. It's in your interests to have a basic familiarity with taxes on both sides of the border. Assuming you can deduct your mortgage interest or rent out your primary residence without carefully tracking the capital gains during the rental period can be a headache if you don't understand the implications ahead of time. Knowing the basics of how cross border taxes work allows you to make informed decisions.

Financial advisors are not the ones on the hook for their mistakes, you are. They benefit by making things seem more complicated than they are.

Most people don't share my enthusiasm for learning about taxes. It's not the dry tax code I find interesting, it's the ability for me to take control of my own financial future I get excited about.

Do I need an accountant?

No, you don't need an accountant to file taxes in both the US and Canada. Do you want to hire one? Maybe, that's up to you. But the point is that it is a choice. All of the information you need to make sound financial decisions and file your taxes is available – for free – from the IRS and CRA.

This guide provides an overview of the issues relevant to those of us who are tax residents of both the US and Canada and points you in the direction to make the decisions that are right for you.

Which country do I pay taxes in?

You usually pay taxes on income in the country you earned it from. If you earn a salary from a Canadian company, they'll deduct taxes from your paycheque and remit them to the CRA.

If you earn a salary from a US company that doesn't have an office in Canada, your taxes will be deducted from your paycheque and remitted to the IRS.

If you have income from multiple sources, you may have income that's taxable on both sides of the border. In nearly all cases, each type of income will only be taxed by one country.

It's easiest to start with doing your taxes for the country that your main source of income is located in. For most of you, that will be Canada. You may have no US based income. In this case, you file your Canadian tax return first. This will give you the final amount you've paid to the CRA and you'll have all of your income and deduction figures ready. Then you can file your US tax return and use the tax exclusions and foreign tax credits to avoid double taxation.

If your primary source of income is in the US, you'll want to file your US tax return first. You'll report all of your income, regardless of its source. This will give you the amount you've paid in taxes to the IRS and you'll have already calculated all of your income and deduction figures. Now you'll file your Canadian tax return and use the foreign tax credits to avoid double taxation. You'll likely owe money for the portion of your provincial taxes that can't be offset by foreign tax credits.

You can't just plug the numbers from one tax return into the other, since the way each number is calculated is a little different for each country. However, by knowing the ways in which they differ, you can make these adjustments quickly and not have to redo your accounting. Of course, don't forget to convert the currency.

Will I pay twice as much in tax?

Absolutely not. You'll end up paying the higher of the two tax rates for each source of income. That's generally the tax rate for Canada and that's where you're living, so there's really no difference between what you'll owe and what someone only filing in Canada would owe.

Sometimes there's something that's taxable in one country and not the other, like a TFSA. Usually you can use foreign tax credits to avoid having to pay this additional tax.

Are taxes higher in Canada?

It's very difficult to say if Canada has higher taxes, because there's no simple comparison. In Canada your taxes include your health insurance costs. In the US your health insurance costs vary widely and are paid in a variety of different ways.

Both countries have hybrid systems, where taxes are raised through income and consumption. The US leaves more employment perks untaxed, while Canada is more likely to tax payments in kind. While tax rates are higher in Canada, US Social Security taxes are significantly higher than the Canadian equivalent, which tends to even this out for people at lower income levels.

They handle corporate taxes very differently, with the US not recognizing corporate taxes paid when shareholders file and Canada providing some integration of corporate and personal taxes through the dividend tax credit.

In my case, I pay about the same amount in taxes while living in Ontario as I paid for taxes and health insurance in New York.

Understanding tax residency

I get asked when I moved to Canada all the time. It's one of those small talk questions and it's surprisingly tricky to answer. Was it the day I declared landed immigrant status? The day I bought my first condo in Toronto? The day my (now ex) wife sold our home in Brooklyn? The day we moved all of our belongings across the border? When I traded in my New York drivers license for an Ontario one? The CRA and IRS recognize that this is a bit of a gray area.

CRA form NR74 can help you make sure the day you decide your residency began, for tax purposes, will be okay with the CRA. For the record, I decided that the day my cat arrived in Toronto was the day it officially became home.

You'll want to file form 8938 to provide the IRS with your new address. However, as long as you have the right to return to the US, as a citizen or permanent resident, you're considered an American tax resident. This is why you have to file in both countries.

Make sure you're no longer a US state resident

Filing a US federal return is mandatory for US citizens, but you may or may not have to file a US state or municipal return.

Every state and municipality has different rules to determine who needs to file income tax returns, so you'll want to check the requirements for the last state and city you lived in before you moved to Canada. If you moved from a US state that doesn't have income taxes and no longer have US-based income, you don't need to worry about it.

Some states require you to take specific actions to demonstrate that you're no longer a resident. You may have to file a form to officially change your tax residency. This is generally referred to as your 'domicile.' Your domicile is your permanent address. You only have one domicile at a time. Don't just stop filing taxes in a state, check the domicile requirements first.

In order to change your domicile, you need to leave your old domicile, physically move to a new locality, and intend to permanently or indefinitely stay in your new location. This is demonstrated by how much time you spend in a place, where you have a home, where your job is located, where your family lives, where you own property, your driver's license, your car registration, the address on your bank accounts, where your children attend school, and where you procure professional services (like going to the doctor). They've even been known to consider the location of cemetery plots.

If I was sent to work in Toronto for two years and knew I'd return to Brooklyn, I'd probably be considered a New York State resident during that time. New York State (and City!) could require me to file and pay taxes for those two years.

Some states require you to pay taxes if you earn money there or spend 183 days a year there, regardless of the location of your domicile. This is especially important if you continue to work for a US-based company.

Even if your state or municipality doesn't require a form, if you're moving from a place that charges income taxes, you may want to include a letter with your last tax return stating that you are no longer a resident and demonstrating that your domicile has changed.

While the federal government recognizes foreign tax credits, state governments may not. Individual US states are not bound by the tax treaty and you may have to pay state income taxes. Check the appendix and with your state to see what situation applies to you.

Michigan, Florida, California, and Massachusetts are known for going after residents who leave the state temporarily or fail to notify the state of their change in domicile. Check the rules for any state and city you've lived in to make sure you're following the rules.

How much time can I spend out of the country and still be a Canadian resident?

Good question! It depends on how long you can legally live in Canada.

Once you have been a resident of Canada for 60 months (aka 5 years), you remain a factual resident until you can prove to the CRA that you have left Canada for good and have no plans to ever move back.

If you're in Canada on a work permit, study permit, or another permit granting you temporary resident status, you stop being a resident once you leave and aren't planning on returning before your permit expires. When you file your final Canadian tax return, you'll need to indicate that you have left Canada and ended your residency.

Once you've made a permanent move to Canada, you can't just accidentally stop being a resident. If you're a permanent resident, you are considered to remain a factual resident of Canada until you've been gone long enough that your PR status expires or you renounce your PR. You can't just move and stop filing your Canadian taxes.

That's right, you can't just move out and be done with it. You have to file a form with the CRA and convince them that you're gone for good. They can reject your claim and continue to consider you a resident.

If you move back to the US temporarily, you simply continue to file taxes in both the US and Canada.

If you temporarily move to a third country where you'd be required to file taxes, make sure they have a tax treaty with both the US and Canada, because you'll need to file in all three countries.

Your provincial health coverage has separate residency requirements, so it's likely your health insurance will lapse before your tax residency changes.

Health insurance while you're outside of Canada

Provincial health coverage generally allows you to leave for up to six months without a gap in coverage, allowing you to take extended visits to the US or anywhere abroad without worrying about losing health insurance. Check with your province or territory before making any plans for extended travel, as each one has different rules.

Beware that if you're injured while you're in the US, provincial health coverage will only pay the "table rates" that they'd pay for in-province care. Given the high healthcare costs in the US, this will likely leave you with a significant bill. As Americans, this shouldn't come as a shock.

If you have supplemental insurance, it may cover you for time in the US. Your credit card may also provide travel insurance. Look into the coverage you have already to make sure you get any necessary additional insurance — and avoid paying for duplicate coverage.

As a US citizen who lived in the US for five or more years, you'll qualify for Medicare once you reach 65. If you qualify for Medicare, you'll need to enroll within seven months of turning 65. Enrollment is not automatic. US citizens who don't enroll in Medicare Part A at age 65 may incur a penalty if they fail to demonstrate they have coverage elsewhere.

Medicare Part A is provided at no cost to those who worked in the US for a decade or more and their spouses. If you or your spouse don't qualify for free Part A, you can still pay for coverage. You may decide Part B is worth paying premiums for, depending on how much time you spend in the US and if you plan on returning to the US eventually.

Medicare Advantage and Part D plans are only valid for people domiciled in the US. You can purchase a state Medigap plan to cover emergency care outside of the US while you are still a US resident and keep it once you've moved abroad.

If you're covered by both provincial health insurance and Medicare, you have the fortune of being able to decide which country is the best place to receive care. It also means that snowbirds can be covered in both countries.

There are requirements to qualify for both provincial coverage and Medicare. Check to make sure you qualify — and to see what actions you need to take in order to register. You may incur monthly or annual charges for health insurance coverage.

What do you need to do to stop filing taxes in Canada?

As a permanent resident or Canadian citizen, you're a factual resident of Canada until you demonstrate to the CRA that you have left Canada permanently. In order to prove this, you'd need to do things like:
- Sell your home or rent it out on a long-term lease
- Move all of your things out of the country (don't leave them in storage in Canada)
- Establish a new home outside of Canada (buy or rent a home)
- Be required to pay taxes in another country
- Get a job with a non-Canadian company or get transferred to a foreign office
- Get a new driver's license in another country
- Give up your Canadian work permit, study permit, or permanent resident status
- Get new health insurance coverage
- Have a reason for any Canadian bank accounts you're keeping open
- Quit your Canadian professional organizations or unions
- Join new community groups abroad

These things aren't hypothetical, the CRA asks about them.

If you leave your spouse and kids behind or don't have to pay taxes to another country, they're going to require you to continue paying taxes on your worldwide income.

The CRA requires that you provide a list of all of your assets so they can make sure you don't commit tax evasion in the future.

The CRA may even ask you to provide them with a copy of your foreign tax return to verify that you've really moved and are really paying taxes elsewhere. Remember that the CRA and IRS share information, so if you're in the US they can easily verify any details you provide.

The CRA isn't kidding around with this. If you don't file they'll contact you, using the information they have on file. If you ignore them, they'll freeze your Canadian bank accounts and can put a lien on your Canadian assets.

What happens when you stop being a factual resident?

If you've been a resident for more than 60 months in the last ten years (5 years in 10 years, but counted one month at a time on a rolling basis) you are subject to the exit tax if you stop being a resident of Canada.

That sounds scary (and punitive!) but it's really not. It's designed to make sure you don't run off without paying capital gains taxes.

For tax purposes, on the day you leave Canada forever (or die) you are considered to have sold everything you own and then re-purchased it at market rate. This changes the cost basis of everything you own and you theoretically owe capital gains taxes on the theoretical proceeds.

It's unusual for people leaving Canada to actually have to pay anything for the exit tax. You don't have to pay capital gains taxes on your primary residence, RRSP, or TFSA and that's where most people have all of their net worth. You're basically just reporting all of your assets and their current value to the CRA and promising to pay any taxes you're required to pay when you eventually sell them.

Canada doesn't tax you on capital gains on your primary residence, but once you move it's not your primary residence anymore. If you keep your former home, you'll need to have it assessed to determine the new cost basis for the eventual capital gains tax determination. It is much easier to do this now then to try to figure out the hypothetical past value when you sell.

If you do have to pay something for the exit tax, you're not paying any extra money, you're just pre-paying a portion of the capital gains taxes you'll eventually owe when you sell. It's very rare for the CRA to not grant requests to defer tax payment until the actual sale. If you make a lot of money now and plan on selling once you retire (and will be in a lower tax bracket) deferring can be advantageous.

If you sell everything before you leave, you're just paying normal capital gains taxes.

Power of attorney and living wills

Lots of people neglect to establish POA, living wills, and end of life care documents until they're terminally ill – if they create them at all. Given how unexpected many critical illnesses, disabilities, and deaths are, it's best to prepare these documents long before you expect to need them.

It's especially important to have your documents in order when your family is divided across borders – or divided by arguments. If you don't want that your healthcare or financial decisions be made by an estranged parent, soon-to-be-ex, or incompetent sibling, put down your choices in writing ahead of time.

Many people have strong feelings about what sort of care they'd like to receive if there's been a serious accident or if they are too ill to make their own health care decisions. Don't force your family to guess – and question the choices they make for the rest of their lives.

Each province and state has its own requirements for a POA or living will to be valid. Technically, most places only require that a POA meet the requirements of the location it was created in. However, whether or not it will be recognized when you need it is a different matter.

Power of attorney and living will templates are available online. Your hospital system is typically happy to help you put this paperwork together using standard forms and will file it in your medical record. It's best to provide these documents to your medical team, attorney, and family members.

If people can't find the paperwork when it matters, you may as well not have done it at all.

Part Two: Tax planning in two countries

Anyone who tells you they're getting taxed twice is either confused about what taxes they're paying or is doing something horribly wrong on their taxes.

While you won't face double taxation, the things that are taxed in each country and the specific rules and rates are different. In instances where the tax rules diverge, you can smooth it out with foreign tax credits and deductions.

By being familiar with the tax code and how it differs in both countries, you can make investment choices that work with your long-term plans.

Tax filing deadlines

If you're living in Canada, it's probably going to be easiest to file your Canadian return first. Once that's done, adjust for differences in the tax code, convert the amounts to US dollars, and file your American tax return.

US taxes are infamous for their complexity. They can get quite convoluted. However, for many Americans living in Canada, the 1040EZ or 1040 is all you need to worry about.

If you're in the position to panic about your tax situation, you probably already have a team of professionals to worry about the details for you.

US tax deadlines

If you mail your tax return from abroad, the postmark date will count as the date of filing. Payments, however, are only recognized the day they are received. If you owe US taxes, you will want to ensure you mail any payments with sufficient time to arrive by the deadline. You can also simply pay online.

If you defer your tax deadline and expect to owe taxes, you should submit your estimated payment by the April 15th deadline or you may end up owing additional interest and penalties.

Most Americans living in Canada will find it easier to file electronically. Electronic payments can be made through a US bank account, US debit or credit card, wire transfer, or some foreign bank accounts.

Americans living abroad are eligible for an automatic 2 month tax extension. This means the April 15th deadline is pushed back to June 15th. To take advantage of this, simply attach a letter listing your address in Canada or write "Taxpayer Resident Abroad" at the top of your tax return. If you owe US taxes, remember you will have to pay interest from April 15th, not the extended deadline.

You can push the deadline back to October 15th by filing form 4868. This automatic extension also applies only to the filing deadline, not the payment deadline. You'll still owe interest and penalties from April 15th.

You can request a further tax extension for special tax treatment using form 2350.

Canadian tax deadlines

Your Canadian T1 is due April 30th. If you're self employed, your taxes aren't due until June 15th. If you're not a resident, but still need to file, you have until June 30th.

Even if you extend your tax deadline, payments are due by April 30th.

Converting currency

You'll need to file your Canadian tax returns in Canadian dollars and your US tax returns in US dollars.

The IRS doesn't have an official exchange rate. As long as you use a posted exchange rate consistently, you'll be fine. Most people seem to use the yearly average exchange rates posted by the IRS. This makes the most sense if you earned your income throughout the year, as you would with a salary. If you earned a large amount of income or incurred a large expense on a single day, you may want to use the exchange rate on that day.

Keeping track of expenses and deductions

I get the impression that lots of people truck boxes of receipts and printed out emails to their accountants each year. If this is what you're doing, there's no need to do this. Do you really want to hang onto all of your home improvement receipts until you sell your house? Both countries accept electronic records.

Much of the work we associate with filing our taxes is really part of the budgeting and small business accounting we should be doing throughout the year. If any of the information on your taxes comes as a surprise – is your side hustle actually losing money? did you get hit with a huge tax bill you weren't anticipating? – you'll want to do a better job of tracking things quarterly. If your side hustles are particularly successful, you'll want to pay quarterly taxes to soften the blow and avoid penalties.

There are lots of tools to help you track expenses. I find that the simplest way is to scan each receipt and save it in Google Drive as soon as I get it. The Google Drive app makes getting a clear PDF as simple as snapping a photo.

There are many ways to take your receipts and get them into a spreadsheet or your accounting software. There is software to automatically read the receipt or services to have someone else type it up for you. Given issues of different currencies, needing to match each receipt to the appropriate expense category, and matching receipts to various client meetings, I find it just as simple to type them up myself. The penance of this tedious task is also good motivation for keeping my business expenses to a minimum.

Missing documents

What happens if you can't obtain copies of a document you need in order to file your taxes? This happens all the time. Employers go out of business and don't provide employees with tax documents. Bitter exes refuse to provide documents. Records are lost or destroyed in floods. Maybe you just don't know where you put them.

If you're unable to get exact information, you're expected to provide estimates that are as accurate as possible. This is a great opportunity to use the algebra you haven't used since school. If the amount of information you're estimating is significant, you'll want to provide a letter of explanation.

I spoke with employees with the IRS and the CRA and they both said this was common and not to worry about it. As long as your estimates represent a good faith effort to be honest, you'll be fine.

US federal taxes

The US offers exclusions and deductions for Americans living abroad. This is a boon to Americans organizing their life around tax avoidance. As an American living in Canada, you'll most likely have enough Canadian foreign tax credit to cover any amount of taxes you may end up owing in the US.

Reading a tax treaty doesn't sound particularly interesting, but perhaps your interest will be piqued since you likely can benefit from it. You can read the full text of the Canada-US tax treaty on the IRS website.

Your spouse

If you're married to someone who is not a US citizen or permanent resident, you'll still need to include them on your taxes. The IRS refers to someone who is not a US tax resident as a non-resident alien (NRA).

Treating your spouse as a resident alien

If it's advantageous to file married filing jointly and your spouse is not a US citizen or permanent resident, you can elect to have them file as a US citizen and claim the foreign earned income tax exclusion. They will have to report their worldwide income.

This is usually helpful when the US spouse earns over $100k and much more than the non-US spouse, allowing them to use the full FEIE for a married couple.

If your spouse has no income from the US, you can claim them as a dependent on your return.

You'll need to get an individual taxpayer identification number (ITIN) for your spouse.

Treating your spouse as a non-resident alien

If your spouse is not a US citizen and they have income not covered by the FEIE, you would not want to treat them as a US citizen for tax purposes. This requires filing as married, filing separately and having them not file US taxes.

If you're married, filing separately, you'll miss out on certain tax deductions. However, this probably won't be an issue because you're unlikely to owe any taxes in the US.

Gifts to your spouse

You can give whatever you want to your spouse in either country without having to pay taxes, with some caveats.

The US provides you an unlimited marital deduction for US citizen spouses. If your spouse is not a US citizen, you can set up a qualified domestic trust.

In Canada, if you're gifting something to a spouse to minimize taxes, attribution rules will cause problems for your plan.

There is also a difference in who counts as a spouse for the IRS and the CRA. If you're legally married, you're fine in both jurisdictions. If you're common law or the US doesn't recognize your marriage, the IRS will view it as a taxable event.

Attribution rules

Accountants like to make a big deal about attribution rules, but it's something few of us need to worry about. They're designed to make it harder for people to avoid paying capital gains taxes on capital property (like land and buildings) by transferring it to family members or trusts.

For whatever reason, a lot of the information online about attribution rules use examples of things that aren't taxable, like spouses jointly selling a primary residence or adding a spouse to the title of a primary residence. Attribution rules are designed to prevent tax evasion, so if you wouldn't owe any taxes (like in the cases of a primary residence, where capital gains aren't taxable) they don't apply.

If you own an apartment building and want to lower your taxes by transferring it into the name of your kid, the CRA does not appreciate your cleverness. They'll use attribution rules to send you the tax bill. Once that's paid, your kid is on the hook for taxes on future earnings. This might still make financial sense, depending on your situation.

If you have a taxable investment account shared with your spouse, the CRA will tax you based on your proportion of the contributions, so you'll want to keep track of this. However, once the property has been transferred, from that point on any income earned is considered secondary income and the recipient will be responsible for taxes. Or, in the case of a joint investment account, you'd now own the investments 50/50 and owe taxes accordingly.

Your salary

Short stays in Canada

If you work for a company in Canada, they're required to withhold taxes from your paycheck. This is required, even if you only work in Canada for a single day during the year!

If you're only planning on working in Canada for a short amount of time (and don't just want to adjust your schedule to make your taxes simpler), you can get an exemption from withholding and remitting.

Your employer can file form R102-R: Regulation 102 Waiver Application at least 30 days before you start working in Canada. Or, if your US employer has sent you to work in Canada for a short time, your employer can file form RC473: Non-Resident Employer Certification to cover all employees for up to two years.

In order to qualify for an exemption, you can't be in Canada for more than 90 days a year. If you're approved, other deductions, like the Canada Pension Plan premiums and Employment Insurance contributions will not have to be withheld. If this is the case, you'll need to pay these taxes in the US. Make sure that your US employer is making these withholdings.

Foreign earned income exclusion

The first $105.9k of income you earn each year through salaries, wages, commissions, bonuses, professional fees, and tips from sources outside of the US is excluded from taxation thanks to the foreign earned income exclusion (FEIE). If you're married, you can exclude $211.8k each year. The FEIE amount increases each year, because it's pegged to inflation.

Use form 2555 or 2555-EZ to calculate your foreign earned income exclusion. You then subtract this amount from your earned income.

Other types of income are not excluded by the foreign earned income tax exclusion.

Earned income	Unearned income	Variable income
Salaries & wages	Dividends	Business profits
Commissions	Interest	Royalties
Bonuses	Capital gains	Rents
Professional fees	Gambling & lottery	Scholarships & fellowships
Tips	Alimony	
	Social Security income	
	Pensions	
	Annuities	

In order to qualify for the FEIE, you need to be a tax resident of another country. This is designed to prevent Americans abroad from owing taxes in two countries, not as a tool to evade taxes by spending the summer in Muskoka.

You must also be either a bona fide resident or have been physically present in another country for at least 330 days during a period of 12 consecutive months. Most people will easily meet the physical presence test. If not, bona fide residency is a little trickier to establish.

Simply traveling outside of the US for the year, like going on a gap year, doesn't make you a non-resident. You have to actually establish residency elsewhere. If your job sends you abroad for a year or less, this is temporary and doesn't qualify for the FEIE. If you're on a short term contract, you probably won't qualify for a FEIE unless your actions make it clear that you intend to stay in your current home abroad when your current contract expires and have a legal pathway to do so.

Even if you don't qualify for the FEIE, you don't have to worry about double taxation. The US will give you a dollar for dollar tax credit for any foreign taxes you've paid.

Bona fide residence

You need to stay in your new home abroad for at least an entire tax year. Once you've established residency you can claim it for part of a year if you move back to the US.

This is where the IRS delves into semantics.
- Your bona fide residence is your primary home.
- Your domicile is your permanent home.
- Your abode is where you regularly live and work.

They can be different and that's okay. This is pretty subjective and the

IRS doesn't provide clear guidelines. They look at your intentions (primarily based on what you do, not just what you say) and the nature and length of your stay abroad.

Your bona fide residence is where you've put down roots, even if you don't plan on spending the rest of your life there.

Let's say you are from Detroit and take a job in Halifax. You get a Nova Scotia drivers license, enroll your kids in school, and generally make your home in Halifax, but you plan on moving back to Detroit eventually. You keep your home in Detroit and spend your holidays there. You're a bona fide resident of Halifax, even if Detroit is your domicile.

Let's say you are from Detroit and take frequent business trips to Halifax. You get an apartment there, but your spouse and kids stay in Detroit and you fly back and forth. Detroit is your residence and your domicile. You don't meet the bona fide residence test.

Before I became a Canadian permanent resident I spent over a year splitting my time between Toronto and Brooklyn. I had an apartment in both cities. However, my cats and my family heirlooms were in Brooklyn. More pertinent to the IRS, I had a New York drivers license in my wallet and used my New York address for everything. I was a New Yorker with a pied-à-terre in Toronto.

Once I became a permanent resident, my wife sold our home in Brooklyn and we kept my apartment in Toronto. I got an Ontario drivers license and started volunteering with local organizations. While I used my dad's New Jersey address or my New York office address for a few things, I didn't have much in the way of personal belongings at either place. I traveled to the US often, but I had a wife and cats waiting for me at home in Toronto. I had declared myself a landed immigrant and had no plans to move back to the US. I became a bona fide resident of Canada, even if I wasn't in the country for 330 days in a 12 month period.

Now I don't actually have an abode. Once my cats died, I decided it would be easier to do my work if I travelled full-time instead of going back and forth to Toronto (my ex-wife worked remotely and likes to travel, the cat's didn't) between research trips. My apartment in Toronto remains my domicile even though it's currently rented out, because I haven't set up a home anywhere else. All of my belongings are in Toronto, even if I do tend to leave things at my dad's to make space in my bag. The way I've set up my long-term plans make it clear that I intend to stay in Canada. I'm still a bona fide resident of Canada.

Foreign housing exclusion

If you max out the FEIE, you'll also qualify for the foreign housing exclusion (FHE). This is included on form 2555. Things are different if you're self employed.

The base amount that you can't include in the FHE is 16% of the maximum FEIE based on the days you lived abroad within the tax year. This is explained by the fact that you would have to pay housing costs anywhere you live. Housing costs above that amount can be deducted, up to a limit.

Generally, you cannot deduct more than 30% of the FEIE unless you live in a particularly expensive city. All major Canadian cities make the list of expensive locations. The current limit for Toronto is $113/day or $41,400/year.

Your housing expenses include fees for obtaining a lease, rent, furniture rental, building maintenance fees, property insurance, repairs, utilities (not phone and cable), and parking spot rentals.

You can't include taxes or interest that are deductible separately, the cost of purchasing a house, home improvements, mortgage payments, cleaning services, buying furniture, or depreciation.

If you take the FEIE, you cannot take the earned income credit or a deduction for moving expenses connected to the excluded income. If you make more than the FEIE, you may be able to deduct a portion of your moving expenses.

State income

Don't assume that you cease to be a resident of a state simply because you've left. Some states, like California, require you to prove that you have left for good. New Jersey has its own version of the exit tax.

Most tax software will automatically fill out your US state return based on your federal filing. This makes things easy and will be correct, but it's worth looking into the options to make sure you're filing in the way that makes the most sense for your situation.

Continuing to earn income in the US

If you've ever lived in one state and worked in another, you've dealt with reciprocal tax agreements before. It's common for employees who live in New Jersey and work in New York or live in Maryland and work in the District of Columbia to pay taxes only to one state (or federal district) and avoid double taxation.

Sometimes HR handles this for you, by withholding taxes for your state of residence instead of the state your employer is located in. In other instances, your taxes are withheld in the state you work in and you use tax credits when you file with your own state in April.

Unfortunately, not all states recognize foreign tax credits. Some only recognize foreign tax credits from Canada and Mexico or certain provinces. If a state doesn't allow itemized deductions, there will be no foreign tax deduction.

Different states treat foreign residents differently. You'll want to research the rules for your state to make sure you're filing correctly and minimize the potential for double taxation.

Foreign earned income exclusion

Some states allow the FEIE when calculating state taxes owed. Other states will require you to add your excluded income back in, but may allow you to apply tax credits to offset this.

One thing to keep in mind is that excluding foreign income is that some states provide refundable credits that you may not qualify for if you've excluded your income or applied as a non-resident.

Alabama, New Jersey, and Pennsylvania don't allow you to avoid double taxation on foreign income at the state level. California does not unless you are able to qualify as a nonresident under safe harbor rules.

Safe harbor provisions

Some states have safe harbor rules that allow people to be treated as nonresidents while they're living abroad for 15-18 months or more. There may be requirements like proof of an employment contract abroad or limits on how many days you can be in state while being claiming safe harbor coverage. If you have income sourced in California, Connecticut, Delaware, Idaho, Maine, Missouri, New York, Oklahoma, Oregon, or West Virginia you'll want to learn about their safe harbor provisions to see if you qualify.

Your freelance and hobby income

If you're making money from a hobby, you're required to declare this in both countries. However, you declare hobby income differently from small business income in the US but not Canada. The big difference between hobby income and small business income in the US, in terms of taxes, is that you cannot deduct a loss from hobby income.

The deciding factor in what counts as a hobby and what counts as a business is if you're doing this primarily for fun or for profit. Would you be doing this if you weren't making money? If you are fulfilling the zeitgeist of following your passion and your business is something you love doing, is there a business plan with a clear intent to be profitable under a capitalist system? The IRS has been known to question businesses that declare losses for more than a few years in a row and re-categorize them as hobbies.

Because Canada does not distinguish between hobby income and business income, you can deduct a loss. Just know that declaring losses can attract the attention of the CRA and they'll apply the profit test. In order to declare a loss, you'll need to show that you're intending to make a profit, qualified to do the work in question, and putting a real effort into doing so.

Your business income

If you have a sole proprietorship or partnership, declaring your income and expenses is fairly straightforward in both countries. The categories and rules for allowable business expenses are slightly different, but they're similar enough that it's not much of a hassle to adjust things for each tax return.

If you have another type of company, your business is large enough that you should work with an accountant to determine the best way to file.

Canadian companies

Incorporating your business gets complicated for dual tax residents. If you own more than 10% of the voting or value of the stock of a private corporation you'll need to file form 5471 and report income on Subpart F.

Investment income and personal service income from a foreign source, calculated on Subpart F, is reported on your 1040 the year it's earned.

Highly paid professionals commonly use corporations to defer income (and income taxes) but this rules that option out.

LLCs

Canada doesn't have LLCs, so in Canada your US LLC will be taxed as if it were a company. This mismatch can lead to double taxation, because you're prevented from using foreign tax credits by the difference in how the entity is recognized. In Canada your LLC income is taxed to you personally, while in the US it's a separate entity. You'll want to form a flow through entity, such as a partnership or sole proprietorship, so you can use tax credits. Keep the IRS restrictions on pass-through income in mind.

Your home and cottage

Home buyer tax credits

The US no longer has a homebuyer tax credit.

Canada does have a first-time home buyers' tax credit. You don't actually have to be a first-time buyer to qualify, you just can't have owned a home (or have lived in a home your spouse owned) for the previous four years. You can also claim the credit if you're disabled.

The home can be a single, semi, townhouse, condo, co-op, or mobile home. It can't be an investment property, you need to actually live in it, and the home needs to be in Canada. This credit is essentially a $750 non-refundable tax rebate. It goes on line 369.

You can get a rebate on the GST/HST on a new home you purchase, regardless of if you've owned a home before. The purchase price must be below C$450k for you to qualify.

If you're a first time home buyer in Ontario, British Columbia, or Prince Edward Island, you can get a rebate on the land transfer tax. Toronto also offers a rebate on the municipal land transfer tax.

If you or a family member have a disability, you can participate in the home buyers' plan (HBP). This allows you to withdraw up to $25k from your RRSP to purchase or build a home to meet your needs.

Mortgage interest deduction

Mortgage interest and points on your primary residence and a vacation home are deductible on your US taxes, regardless of where in the world it's located. Of course, you're bound by the same restrictions as you would be if the property were in the US.

Mortgage interest on a personal use property is not tax deductible in Canada.

Mortgages in Canada

In the US, a fixed rate mortgage locks in the rate for the entire duration of the mortgage, which is often 30 years. In Canada, fixed rate mortgages renew every five years (or less), so the rate will change.

Mortgages in both countries stipulate rules about payments in excess of the minimum. In the US, you can generally pay off your mortgage in full when you sell the property and not face any penalty. In Canada, this is usually not the case. Ending a mortgage early to sell a property is considered breaking a mortgage and there may be costs involved, typically based on the interest you would have paid had you kept the mortgage for the full term.

Capital gains taxes on your home

People make a big fuss about the US charging capital gains tax on your primary residence while Canada doesn't. Much like if someone is complaining about having to pay US taxes on their Canadian salary, if someone is complaining about paying US capital gains taxes on their home sale, I hope they're picking up the bill when you hang out, because they made a lot of money.

If you live in your home the entire time you own it and only own one home, it is unlikely that you will owe capital gains taxes in either country. In the US, the first $250k of capital gains ($500k if you're married) is tax-free. That's not the total sale price, that's the amount of profit that's tax exempt.

Canada doesn't require you to pay capital gains tax on the sale of your primary residence, but it has much more stringent requirements for what qualifies as a primary residence. In the US you only have to live in the home for two out of the five years before the sale.

This gets tricky if you claimed depreciation on any portion of your home, such as if you've rented out a basement apartment or had a home office. That portion of your home is considered an investment property. Most people who rent out part of their primary residence seem to opt to not claim depreciation to keep things simple.

We're talking about capital gains here. If you owned your home for less than a year, the whole tax structure of your sale changes. Then you're in the business of flipping houses.

Capital gains taxes in Canada

You don't pay capital gains taxes in Canada on the sale of your primary residence, but that's only for the years it's your primary residence. You will owe taxes on the gains for any time you rent out your home (or simply have it as your non-primary residence). This is because changing the use of your home is considered deemed disposition.

If you decide to rent out your home, this changes the use and it isn't your primary residence for those years. You'll want to figure out your adjusted cost basis at that time. The increase in value during its time as a rental property will be considered taxable capital gains, while its increase during its time as your primary residence is not taxable. You can get a fair market value report from an appraiser or a Realtor.

If you're married, you and your spouse can only claim one home as your primary residence. If you're marrying someone and you both own a home, you'll want to get an adjusted cost basis on whichever home you decide will not be your primary residence for use when you sell the properties.

If you get divorced, your home is considered to remain your primary residence so long as one of you is still living there.

In Canada, you are required to report the sale of your home, even if you are exempt from capital gains taxes on the sale.

Renting out your primary residence and electing to maintain primary residence status

If you're renting out your home temporarily, you can get permission from the CRA to have it remain your primary residence. If your job transfers you, you can rent it out as long as you stay with the same employer. Otherwise, you can make this election for up to four years.

During this time you can't establish another primary residence (since you can only have one for each year) and you must remain a factual resident of Canada (because otherwise you can't have a primary residence in Canada at all).

You still have to declare your rental income and can't claim a capital cost allowance on the property.

This means you can rent out your home while you live with family, travel, or rent in another city without changing the tax status of your home.

Capital gains taxes in the US

If you have lived in your home for 24 months out of the previous 60 months, you can exclude gains of up to $250k US on your taxes. This is per person, so if you're married that number bumps up to $500k. In order to claim the married exemption, you will need to file jointly. You can only claim the exclusion for one home in any two year period.

If you need to sell your home and don't meet the exemption requirements, check the specific IRS rules, because you may still qualify. Being transferred for work and other scenarios are written into the rules.

If you make enough profit on the sale of your home that you exceed the exclusion, only the amount above the exclusion is taxed. You can use foreign tax credits to offset this.

If you have a spouse who is not a US tax resident and a house outside of the US that you anticipate will make you more than $500k in profits when you sell, you can transfer the property to them and avoid the issue with US taxes entirely. This is where it's wise to think about your financial future in advance, since transferring the property immediately before the sale is tax evasion, while doing it when you first notice the market rising is tax planning.

In the US, you are not required to report the sale of your home if you are exempt from capital gains taxes on the sale.

Calculating the cost basis

The cost basis for a property, like your primary residence, includes not just the amount what you paid for the property, but also the expenses of actually buying and selling it, as well as any improvements you made.

When calculating the cost basis, you need to convert the currency based on the exchange rate at the time of the transaction, not the sale date. This can mean your capital gains are different in the US and Canada, resulting in a phantom gain or loss.

This is most relevant if you have a mortgage on the property. The exchange rate changes the difference between how much money you originally took out as a loan and how much money you actually paid back, since you're reporting this to the IRS in USD and the CRA in CAD. This currency rate exchange loss or gain is considered personal property and the IRS will not allow you to deduct the loss. If you made money on the currency exchange, it does factor into your capital gains.

Before you pull out your calculator and start figuring out if you made a profit on the fluctuating currency rates, make sure the math is even relevant. Do some quick math on estimated numbers to see if you're likely to have made a profit in the amount over the capital gains tax exclusion first. If you qualify for the tax exclusion and you're within the amount, there's no need to determine your exact profit.

Renting out part of your home

If you rent out more than 50% of your home and/or claim capital cost allowance (known as depreciation south of the border) on the part of your home that you're renting out, your ability to exempt your home from capital gains taxes gets complicated.

If you have a multi-family home and live in one of the units, you'll treat the portion of the home that was your unit as your primary residence and the remainder as an investment property.

Your old home in the US

Once you move to Canada, your home in the US will become a second home or investment property.

You can still claim this capital gains tax exemption if a home was your primary residence for two of the five years before the sale, so you have three years after you move to sell your old home and avoid capital gains taxes. There are special exemptions to the capital gains tax exemption requirement to live in your home for two years, such as needing to move for work, so if you don't think you qualify, double check before you pay taxes.

The cost basis of your home does not change in the US when you convert it from your primary residence to a rental property. If you live in your home for 20 years and rent it for 4, you'll have to pay capital gains on the full amount. If you rent it for only 3, you'll be able to utilize the capital gains tax exemption.

Gifting your home

People claim that Canada doesn't have a gift tax, but they have a deemed disposition tax which amounts to the same thing. If you transfer the title of a property to someone else (like a family member) you'll owe capital gains taxes as if you'd sold it for fair market value. However, in most cases this will be negated by the capital gains tax exclusion.

Cross border trusts

Many financial advisors will suggest creating a cross border trust (CBT) if you own property in both countries that you would like to leave to a non-dual citizen spouse or other family members. This allows your property to avoid probate and minimize taxation. If you're interested in this option, you should speak to a professional.

Your investment property

If you have a foreign investment property with an adjusted cost basis of C$100k or more, or several with a cumulative value over this total, you'll need to file form T1135 each year. This can be done online. This is only required for investment properties, not vacation homes or any property not intended to earn income.

When selling an investment property, you'll have to report the capital gains to both countries, regardless of where in the world it's located. Thanks to tax credits, you will only need to pay taxes on it in one country.

If you were only reporting your income in the US, you could move into an investment property for two years before you sell and take the primary residence capital gains exemption. This trick doesn't work in Canada, so you'll want to use capital losses to offset your gains, if possible.

Deferring taxation

In Canada, businesses can defer capital gains in some instances. This is most commonly used for businesses that need to upgrade their facilities or move their office to a new location. You can do things like trade one warehouse for another without triggering a taxable event.

In the US, you can defer capital gains taxes using a like kind exchange, commonly known as a 1031 exchange. You can identify a similar property to the one you're selling within 45 days and close on it within 180 days of the sale and defer capital gains taxes. You can keep doing this each time you sell, so long as the new purchase qualifies.

Because the 1031 exchange is not recognized by both countries, if you use it you'll have a radically different cost basis in each country for the same property.

It's important to note that things like the 1031 don't eliminate capital gains taxes, they just defer them. Theoretically, paying capital gains taxes now or later shouldn't make a difference in how much you pay. If you pay now, you update the cost basis of the property to include the gain. If you defer it, you'll eventually owe taxes on the gains from the cost basis of the original property.

If capital gains taxes are deferred long enough, decades of depreciation must be recaptured and the taxes may grow so high as to create a tax loss even on a profitable sale. The most financially prudent option becomes offloading it to a charity.

Capital gains taxes on investment properties

If you claimed depreciation on your investment property, known as the capital cost allowance (CCA) in Canada, this will be recaptured and taxed, along with the capital gains. Claiming depreciation is mandatory in the US, but not in Canada. Even if you claim depreciation in both countries, the depreciation schedule differs in each.

In Canada, 50% of the capital gains are taxable at your marginal tax rate. That 50% number is not the tax rate you pay, it's giving you half of your capital gains tax free. You also only pay capital gains when you sell the property (or leave Canada forever or die), while most other types of income are taxed when you earn it. Estate planning aims to defer capital gains indefinitely.

You can use capital losses (selling investments for less than you bought them for) to offset capital gains (selling investments for more than you bought them for).

Your disability income

The Canada Pension Plan (CPP) and Quebec Pension Plan (QPP) both provide disability coverage. You qualify if you've worked for 4 of the past 6 years, or 3 of the past 6 years if you've worked at least 25 years. If you don't meet the requirements for disability income in Canada, the US-CA Totalization Agreement can help you qualify for benefits by giving you credit for time worked in the US.

If you qualify for Social Security Disability benefits in the US, you can continue to collect them while a resident of Canada. You can still apply for disability benefits in the US after you've left.

Many employers offer disability benefits. Check with your HR department to see what kind of coverage you might have. If you don't have coverage or have gaps in your coverage, you can purchase private disability insurance. You may also want to purchase long-term care insurance. Be sure any insurance policies you purchase will fit with your plans, especially if you anticipate retiring outside of Canada.

Government retirement plans

With Canada's immigration system weighted to favor the young, few newcomers look into how their US Social Security benefits will transfer, how to manage their current retirement accounts in the US, or how the move will impact their disability coverage.

If you're in that sliver of the population who wants to make sure your ducks are in a row for the future, here's what you need to know.

Canada has the Canada Pension Plan (CPP), Quebec Pension Plan (QPP), and Old Age Security (OAS). They're the Canadian versions of Social Security (SS) in the US.

Before you start to get nervous, the US and Canada recognize contributions to each other's government retirement plans. Contributions you've made to Social Security in the US will count towards CPP and QPP in Canada.

Before you get excited, if you apply to receive both CPP/QPP/OAS and Social Security, your payments will be reduced by the "windfall elimination provision." I'm not sure who thinks OAS+SSI is a 'windfall', but clearly someone does and they're going to keep you from gaming the system.

Canadian retirement plans

So long as you work for at least one year, you'll qualify for CPP or QPP. Service Canada can provide you with an estimate of your future payments. There is no payment for spouses who did not contribute to the system, but you can split payments with your spouse.

Old Age Security is determined solely on how long you've lived in Canada, not your contributions. You'll need to have lived in Canada for 20 years after your 18th birthday in order to qualify for OAS. Once you qualify, Canada will recognize years you've lived in the US as counting towards your total. You'll qualify for maximum OAS benefits if you've lived in Canada and/or the US for 40 years as an adult.

Right now, the average annual combined CPP and OAS income is a little over $15k a year.

If you make over a certain amount, your OAS benefits are reduced. This is officially known as the OAS recovery tax, but it's known as the clawback.

If you are receiving OAS while no longer a Canadian tax resident and living in a country with a tax treaty, like the US, you don't have to submit the Old Age Security Return of Income (OASRI) form and aren't subject to the clawback.

Social Security

You can still qualify for Social Security, regardless of where in the world you live. American retirees living abroad can happily confirm that Social Security will direct-deposit your SSI each month.

If you left the US before you qualified for Social Security, you can apply your contributions to the CPP or QPP in order to qualify. Social Security provides benefits to spouses (or ex-spouses, depending on how long you were married) who did not directly contribute to the system.

Your SS payments are proportional to your average top earnings over 35 years, adjusted for inflation. You may be surprised by how much you get after only working a few years -- or how little you get after working many. Your social security account online can provide an estimated payment amount based on your work history.

Your tax-sheltered accounts

The US and Canada have tax treaties for retirement accounts, but they don't include all tax sheltered accounts. There's a lot of conflicting information out there about reporting requirements for accounts not mentioned in the tax treaty. That's because the IRS hasn't issued instructions.

Accountants like to take the most conservative approach, even when it involves jumping through unnecessary hoops. The IRS hasn't said a TFSA is a foreign trust, but some accountants thinks that might be what it is based on old court cases. There isn't a consensus, so you'll have to use your own judgement.

When the IRS doesn't provide instructions on how to report income on an account that's tax sheltered in Canada, you have to make a best faith effort to report it correctly. If you write a letter to the IRS the first year you report the account in question detailing the type of account and how you're reporting it asking for guidance, you'll either get an answer on how to report it (unlikely) or be able to demonstrate good faith if you ever get audited.

401k & 403b

If you have access to a US-based 401k or a Canada-based employer retirement savings plan (RSP), you can contribute to that and both countries will recognize the tax sheltered nature of the accounts.

If you have an old 401k or 403b in the US that you can no longer contribute to, the power of compound interest still works. If you have a legacy 401k or 403b from a former employer, check the fees.

You may be able to save a significant amount by moving your money from your old employer plan into a Rollover IRA somewhere with lower fees. It's also typically a lot easier to manage your funds. It can be very difficult to find an investment firm that will accept an American living abroad, so you want to do this before you move.

You can't just withdraw the money from your old retirement plan and move it to an IRA. You'll need to work with both your old and new plan administrators to roll things over without triggering a tax penalty. This is usually pretty simple, but it varies depending on the companies you're dealing with.

Traditional IRA & Roth IRA

In the US, many people have individual retirement plans (IRAs). An IRA is a way for people to make tax-deductible retirement contributions without them needing to be connected to a company plan.

However, there are two issues with IRAs:
- You can only contribute $6k a year, which isn't really enough to save for retirement
- You can only contribute if you have earned income that's taxable in the US that year

In order to contribute money to an IRA, it has to meet two criteria:
- Taxable in the US
- Earned (ie. come from wages, a salary, tips, professional fees or bonuses)

If you've made more than the foreign earned income tax exclusion amount, the first $6k of taxable income can go into a traditional IRA, tax-free. Just remember that you can't contribute more than the amount of taxable income you've earned.

If you don't have earned income that's taxable in the US, you can't contribute to an IRA. If your spouse has earned income in the US and you don't work, they can contribute to an IRA for you.

Even if you can't contribute to your IRA in a given year, your IRA growth isn't taxable in either country.

SEP IRA

If you're self employed or work for a company with fewer than 100 employees, you can have a SEP IRA. The employer (that's you, if you're self employed) has to make the contributions. All eligible employees have to be enrolled and everyone gets the same contribution percentage.

You can contribute 25% of your salary, up to $56k, to a SEP IRA. You can have a SEP IRA as well as a Roth or traditional IRA.

The CRA (and the IRS) give this favorable tax treatment like with a traditional IRA.

Simple IRA

Employers with less than 100 employees can set up a Simple IRA. It has no reporting requirements for companies, so many small businesses choose this type of retirement plan.

You direct your investments, giving you more choices than a 401k through your employer. You can contribute 100% of your income, up to $12,500. That's still less than you can contribute to a traditional 401k, but it's much more than a regular IRA.

Employers are required (mostly) to match your contributions, up to 3%. If you don't contribute, they still have to give you 2%.

The CRA (and the IRS) give this favorable tax treatment like with a traditional IRA.

Solo 401k

If you have income from self-employment that's taxable in the US and no full-time employees, you can set up a Solo 401k. You can make contributions both as the employee and the employer. You can contribute up to 100% of your self-employment earnings, up to $24,000. You can also contribute 25% of your compensation as the employer.

The CRA (and the IRS) give this favorable tax treatment like with a traditional 401k. If your Solo 401k has $250k USD or more you need to file form 5500-SF.

Moving your US retirement accounts to Canada

There is no need to move your retirement accounts out of the US.

You can continue to access your retirement accounts from Canada (or anywhere in the world) although sometimes online banking tools aren't designed for expats. As an American living in Canada, but earning a salary in the US, I fall into an online banking purgatory.

It is possible to roll over your US retirement accounts into Canadian retirement accounts. However, if this is done improperly, you'll have to pay taxes on them as if you'd cashed them out. Also, it's a huge hassle.

If your 401k or 403b balance is below the minimum for it to remain open, it's far easier to roll it into an IRA in the US than move it across an international border. This is a common move and your plan administrator will know how to do it.

Rolling a US retirement plan into an RRSP is much less common, which means an inexperienced administrator is more likely to make a mistake and you will be the one to (literally) pay for it.

If you decide to move your US retirement accounts to Canada, rolling over will create RRSP room for whatever amount you transfer. You will claim this amount as income on your Canadian taxes and use the RRSP deduction to negate the taxes you would otherwise owe. If, for some horrible reason, the IRA withdrawal and RRSP deposit don't happen in the same tax year, you face a tax nightmare.

The details are tricky, so talk to your plan administrator about the tax implications you would face and what you need to do. Or, take the easy road and just leave your US retirement accounts in the US.

Discussing moving US bank and investment accounts to Canada is the only time an investment advisor will ever mention currency risk. Normally they encourage you to diversify your investments for safety, but suddenly in this case they view having your retirement in two different currencies as a risk! This is extra preposterous given the popularity of US dollar accounts in Canada.

Canadian investment firms are known for having fewer investment choices, limited reporting on performance results, and higher fees than US investment firms. Further, most advisors in Canada are paid on commission.

If you make contributions to your US retirement plans while you were a Canadian resident, you can't roll it over into an RRSP.

You cannot convert an RRSP into an IRA. The retirement accounts only go north.

RRSP

The Canadian version of a traditional IRA is a registered retirement savings plan (RRSP). This allows Canadian residents to save 18% of their last year's earned income, up to around $26k. RRSP contributions are tax deductible and their gains are tax-deferred. If you withdraw money from your RRSP before retirement it will probably earn you a tax penalty.

Contributions to an RRSP aren't allowed for the first year that you file a tax return in Canada, since you haven't established any contribution room yet. Your Notice of Assessment from the CRA will show your contribution room. It's also shown on your myCRA account. If you don't make the full allowable contribution, you can roll it over into a future year. Unused contribution room can be very helpful if you get a large payment that would otherwise be taxable.

You can also contribute $2k over your allowance during your lifetime. You'll have to pay taxes on that $2k, but all future income from that overage will continue to grow tax-free.

Spouses can open RRSPs for each other, which is great if one of you makes significantly more money.

If you make less than $40k a year, you won't benefit much from the tax savings. However, it's always good to save, even if you're not getting great tax perks. If you're feeling brave, you can save this contribution room for years when you're in a higher tax bracket.

The US will recognize the tax-sheltered nature of an RRSP.

PRPP

If you're self-employed or work for a small business and don't have access to a workplace pension plan, you can now enroll in a pooled registered pension plan (PRPP). Not everyone is eligible to participate.

Your RRSP contribution room determines how much you can contribute to your PRPP. The contribution room is shared across both your PRPP and your RRSP.

Once you have a PRPP, it's tied to your SIN, so you take it with you when you switch employers.

The PRPP was only introduced in 2011, so it was not included in the tax treaty. However, it's likely that a PRPP would be considered as a pension plan or RRSP by the IRS.

RRIF

Once you retire, you move your RRSP funds into a Registered Retirement Income Fund (RRIF). You must convert your RRSP to an RRIF by the age of 71 and begin making minimum withdrawals. If you have multiple RRSPs, you can consolidate them into one RRIF.

You cannot contribute to a RRIF and investment income remains tax deferred. There's an annual minimum withdrawal amount, but no maximum.

While your withdrawals are taxed, your minimum amount is tax free. If you don't have a pension, you may qualify for additional tax free withdrawals.

Your bank will likely allow you to set up scheduled payments, if you'd like to get a paycheque like you're used to.

You can base your age for RRIF purposes on your spouse's age. If you die and leave your RRIF to your spouse, they can convert it back to an RRSP if they're young enough.

The US will recognize the tax-sheltered nature of an RRIF.

IPP

An Individual Pension Plan (IPP) is benefits high earning owners of incorporated businesses and senior executives. Your contributions are based on your age and income.

TFSA

A Tax Free Savings Account (TFSA) is like a Roth IRA. Contributions aren't tax deductible, but all investment income is tax free when you withdraw it.

You get a standard amount of contribution room each year, regardless of your income level. This room adds up, so you can make contributions for past years when you have the money.

Unlike a Roth IRA, you can withdraw money at any time, assuming it's allowable by the investment you've made (things like CDs/GICs have their own restrictions). You don't lose room if you withdraw money, so you can re-contribute what you withdrew.

You can't open a TFSA for your spouse, but you can give them money to contribute to theirs.

TFSAs aren't included in the US-CA tax treaty. Why? They were only created in 2009, after the most recent treaty updates. Thus, you'll owe US taxes on any earnings in a TFSA. However, if you have tax credits, you could use them to make up for the tax difference.

The IRS has said nothing about how to report a TFSA. Some tax advisors claim you'll need to file form 3520 or Form 3520-A with the IRS, treating it as a foreign trust. A TFSA acts less like a trust than an RRSP, which isn't considered a trust by the IRS, so this seems unnecessary.

Some advisors believe that a TFSA should be classified as a foreign disregarded entity, requiring form 8858.

Others say you just need to report the income like with any other investment account. The TFSA has a lot in common with a Roth IRA.

As long as the IRS chooses not to release guidance on this, you should be fine as long as you report it. If you want to be safe, you can write the IRS a letter asking them how to file and stating how you plan on reporting the income and they will ignore you, but you'll be considered compliant.

Because TFSAs are so new, it's likely that they'll be included in any updates to the tax treaty or the IRS will eventually provide more information. It's possible that they will become tax sheltered in the US before you withdraw funds. But, of course, you'll be paying taxes on the earnings until then.

You're not losing anything by putting your investments in a TFSA rather than a regular account, since the US taxes them both at the same rate, so you can go ahead and open a TFSA and hope the IRS adds these to the tax treaty in the future. In the meantime, you can use foreign tax credits to offset any taxes you might owe on the income or accumulate credits for any taxes you're paying on your TFSA income in the US.

RESP

A Registered Education Savings Plan (RESP) allows you to save for tuition and living expenses for students. Earnings are tax sheltered in Canada. The student is responsible for taxes when they're withdrawn, which means they likely will owe no tax, since they probably aren't earning any money. Plans can be set up for an individual child or the family. You can also set up an RESP for your own education costs. In fact, you can set up an RESP for anyone, it doesn't have to be a family member.

The government may add to your contributions, up to $500 a year, with the Canada Education Savings Grant (CESG).

The tax treaty doesn't recognize RESPs. If you have an RESP, some tax advisors will tell you to treat it like a trust and file form 3520 or Form 3520-A with the IRS. Like with a TFSA, it's unclear if this is necessary.

RDSP

A Registered Disability Savings Plan (RDSP) allows you to save for living and medical expenses. The beneficiary needs to be younger than 60. Investment income is only taxed in Canada when it's withdrawn.

You can contribute a lifetime maximum of $200k, with no annual limit. The Canadian Disability Savings Grant and Canada Disability Savings Bond can add to your contributions. The amount in your RDSP doesn't impact OAS or the Guaranteed Income Supplement.

The tax treaty doesn't recognize RDSPs. If you have an RDSP, some tax advisors will tell you to treat it like a trust and file form 3520 or Form 3520-A with the IRS. Like with a TFSA and an RESP, it's unclear if this is necessary.

Your stocks, bonds, and mutual funds

Individual brokerage accounts

Financial investments like stocks, bonds, and mutual funds are still a good bet, even if they aren't tax sheltered.

If you have an individual brokerage account in the US, they may take issue if you add a Canadian address. It seems easy enough to simply use the US address of a family member or friend, but this may end up giving you trouble. When a brokerage issues a 1099, it goes to you, the federal government, and the state government. You may eventually hear from the state and have to battle it out to prove you shouldn't owe state taxes on your investment income.

You may find it easier to set up a brokerage account in Canada, which will still allow you to purchase US stocks.

Canadian mutual funds

Supposedly, US citizens used to use foreign mutual funds to gain tax deferral on undistributed income. In 2010, the IRS declared Canadian mutual funds to be considered corporations for US tax purposes. If you receive income from a passive foreign investment company (PFIC) or sell a mutual fund that's a PFIC, you may owe US taxes and have to file extra forms related to PFICs. The situation is unclear, as the IRS hasn't outlined an official policy, but most financial advisors will tell you to simply avoid them.

You'd have to file form 8621: Return by a Shareholder of a Passive Foreign Investment Company or Qualifying Electing Fund. This form makes you choose between the Qualified Electing Fund (QEF) and the Mark-to-Market Election.

If you choose the QEF, you have to declare your pro rata share of the mutual fund's ordinary earnings as ordinary income and any net capital gain as a long-term capital gain in your annual.

If you take the Mark-to-Market election, you have to declare the annual gain or loss of the shares as if you'd sold them as part of your ordinary income.

This all sounds very complex, and it is, but your brokerage will give you tax documents that provide these numbers for you.

If you hold a Canadian mutual fund that's a PFIC within an RRSP, you don't have to worry about this, because retirement plan gains are taxed as pension income in both countries.

Non-PFIC Canadian mutual funds

Not all Canadian mutual funds are PFICs. While you may choose to steer clear of them for simplicity's sake, you can also choose your investments wisely and still avoid PFICs.

Canadian mutual fund trusts can choose to be classified as partnerships or corporations for US tax purposes by filing a few forms. Given the number of US tax residents investing in Canada, many funds are taking these steps.

Older Canadian mutual fund trusts can either be partnerships or corporations automatically. If not all investors have limited liability, it's a partnership. Most mutual funds created before 2004 were partnerships for US tax purposes and remain so unless their structure has changed. Partnerships are not PFICs and don't require form 8621.

Mutual funds that are not reporting issuers under securities legislation don't have limited liability, meaning they may not be PFICs.

Qualified small business shares

In Canada, qualified small business shares can be exempted from capital gains. The IRS does not have these exemptions, so your gains would be taxable in the US.

Canadian holding companies

If you're a shareholder in a private Canadian corporation that's bringing in a significant amount of passive income, it's considered a PFIC or a controlled foreign corporation. Either way, you face an unfavorable tax situation and extra forms to submit to the IRS.

If you have a Canadian holding company in your portfolio, someone's given you bad financial advice and you should find a new wealth manager.

Your inheritance

Inheriting money from someone in the US or Canada is fairly straightforward, so long as you inherit the money through a will.

The US and Canada each treat the cost basis of property in a trust differently. In the US, the cost basis steps up when the person who created the trust dies. In Canada, the original cost basis is retained. This creates a discrepancy between the amount of tax owed in each country. If you have a trust, the person who manages it can help you determine the best way to plan for this.

Other types of income

Lottery winnings are not taxable in Canada, but they are in the US.

If you are given a gift valued at over $100k by a non-resident alien, you'll need to report this to the IRS on form 3520.

Taxes based on adjusted gross income

Net Investment Income Tax

The US Net Investment Income Tax is a 3.8% tax on individuals, estates, and trusts with income over $200k for individuals or $250k for married couples. The sale of your primary residence does not count toward this number. These numbers are based on your AGI and are not indexed to inflation.

Nonresident Aliens are exempt from the NIIT. If you are a resident of a foreign country for tax purposes and filing using the tax treaty, you are considered a NRA for NIIT.

There is a special rule for NRAs who are treated as resident aliens because they are married to US citizens and filing jointly.

Foreign tax credits and deductions

On the US side, tax credits are usually applied based on the type of income. A credit is used to offset taxes owed on that same sort of income: active, passive, etc. If you can't apply a tax credit for foreign taxes paid, you can use a foreign tax deduction instead or roll it over for future years.

Your estate

Both Canada and the US have an estate tax, which apply to your worldwide assets.

I know, you're saying that Canada doesn't have an estate tax. That's technically true, but they have a deemed disposition tax, which you pay when you die. Like with the exit tax (where you declare yourself dead to Canada), when you die, you're taxed as if all of your investments are sold.

You can call it whatever you want, but that sounds like an estate tax to me. Or death tax, if you're adamantly against it all.

These capital gains are included in your final income tax return (which you won't be filing, since you'll be dead). The cost basis used to calculate capital gains is adjusted to the fair market value at the time of your death, so these assets won't be taxed twice on the same gains.

If you're concerned about your heirs having to sell assets you want them to be able to keep (like the cabin you built outside of Canmore), make sure you're leaving them enough liquid assets (like stocks and bonds) to cover any capital gains taxes they might owe. You can also set up a trust or get a life insurance policy. This is also a good reason to keep organized records of things that impact your cost basis on major assets.

The US has an estate tax, but there's currently an exemption of $11 million. If that's not enough for you, it's set to phase out entirely by 2023.

Your executor

Since you can't file your own taxes once you're dead, this responsibility is left up to your executor. If you have a will, you can choose who you want to carry this out. If you don't name someone, someone will be appointed.

Any CPP or OAS payments received after the month of your death will need to be returned, as will any future GST/HST credits. If you have a spouse, GST/HST credits, CCTB, UCCB, and Canada Child Benefits can be redirected to them.

Your executor will file a return for the months you were living as well as annual returns for your estate until the estate is resolved.

Estates that go through probate frequently take a year or more to sort out, even without anything being contested.

Your spouse

In the US, the IRS only recognizes your spouse if they are a US tax resident or elect to file taxes as a US tax resident. If you are married to a non-resident alien, they are subject to gift tax rules. You can learn more on 26 USC section 2503 (b).

If you die before your (US tax resident) spouse, they can inherit your IRAs, RSP, RRSP, 401k, etc. without taxes. If you own property as joint tenants, property will bypass probate and transfer to the surviving owner.

Your spouse doesn't have to pay the deemed disposition tax on anything they inherit from your estate. Technically, they will have to pay the deemed disposition tax if they sell the assets, however, that's just a way to make paying normal capital gains taxes sound extra complicated.

If you have capital losses or own shares in a qualified small business corporation, farm, or fishing property, it may be best for your spouse to choose to pay deemed disposition now and use these to offset any capital gains.

You can transfer property to your spouse without paying taxes before you die, but because the deemed disposition tax is really just capital gains taxes, it doesn't actually change the tax situation. It does make your lives less complicated when dealing with probate, assuming you know which one of you is going to go first. Or, you can just own the property as joint tenants with survivorship rights.

Your real estate attorney can help you decide how to set things up in the way that makes the most sense for your situation.

Your heirs

Retirement accounts and property left to other family members or friends will be subject to taxation. Heirs generally pay taxes on 50% of the capital gains of stocks, bonds, real estate, and anything else at the personal income tax rate. That means they pay half as much in taxes on this as they would if they'd earned it as a salary.

If you'd like to minimize the amount of taxes you owe and plan on leaving your assets to people with a lower marginal tax rate (or you just don't care how much they'll owe on things you're giving them), you can use an estate freeze. This will step up the cost basis and attribute the value of future growth (and taxes owed) to your heirs.

Avoiding probate

The easiest way to reduce the amount of assets that must go through probate, or eliminate it altogether, is by setting up transfer-on-death accounts. Your bank and investment firm will likely have a simple process for you to set this up for each account.

You can set up joint tenancy with right of survivorship with anyone, not just your spouse. You can set up joint tenancy for real estate, stocks, vehicles, and bank accounts. You'll be giving them ownership to half the property immediately and it will become theirs upon your death. This may trigger gift reporting requirements, depending on the specifics of your relationship and the assets you're transferring.

Gifts

One common way to reduce the size of an estate is to give things to your heirs before you die. In Canada, gifts made within three years of your death are clawed back and included as part of the estate. However, this is mostly a moot point.

In Canada, the gift and estate tax rates are the same. This makes the timing of asset transfer to heirs a matter of personal choice, rather than a tax issue.

In the US, you can give $15k a year to someone without having to declare it to the IRS. This amount is per recipient and per person, so you and your spouse can give up to $30k a year to each recipient.

If you give a gift worth more than that amount, you just need to file form 709, you don't necessarily have to pay any taxes. Form 709 allows the IRS to calculate how much of your lifetime exemption you've used and therefore how much is left for your estate to use when the time comes.

If you're contributing to a 529 plan, paying for a wedding, or covering someone's rent, you might want to spread it out and split it between you and your spouse to avoid using your exclusion. In some circumstances, you can spread one-time gifts across five years.

In the case of paying medical bills or tuition, paying bills directly can help you avoid having this count as a gift for tax purposes.

Remember that the ghost interest on interest-free loans is considered a gift. If you lend someone money and then forgive the loan, that's also a gift as far as the IRS is concerned. If you sell something for less than fair market value (FMV), the difference between FMV and the purchase price is considered a gift.

Having a family member add you to their bank account can also trigger gift taxes. If your family decides to add you to grandma's accounts to make it easier for you to help her manage her finances, the IRS may view that as a taxable event. This is assuming, however, that your grandma has more than $30k in whatever account(s) she's adding you to. In that case, it's certainly worth it to set up a proper financial POA for you and grandma.

Planned giving

Charitable donations can help reduce your estate taxes, especially in the case of real estate where a profitable sale would require re-paying considerable amounts of depreciation.

Making these gifts to charity during your lifetime will reduce your taxes during your life and reduce your executor fees and probate costs once you pass. It also reduces the potential for family members to end up bickering over your will.

Your will

You'll want to make sure your will is legal in both countries, as well as any other countries you hold assets in. You'll want to ensure the same will is filed in both jurisdictions. Contradictory wills across borders will be a nightmare for your family to sort out after your death. Be sure any beneficiaries listed in your retirement and brokerage accounts match the beneficiaries listed in your will.

Any beneficiaries you've named with your bank or investment firm for your 401k, IRA, RRSP, or other accounts will hold precedence over what you have in your will. Be sure to keep these up to date as things in your life change.

If you're concerned about transferring your estate to heirs, you'll want to look into this fully to understand your options and how your residency will impact your tax situation.

Setting up a trust

Moving assets from your name into a trust is one way to minimize the amount of capital gains owed by your estate. This is because the trust won't be part of your estate, so you can continue to defer capital gains.

Transferring property into a trust is a taxable event. Any capital gains tax owed will have to be paid at that point. For a property that's been your primary residence, you won't owe capital gains tax at the time of transfer, but you may owe land transfer taxes.

There will also be the cost of setting up and maintaining the trust.

There are also issues with any retained use of assets in the trust by the original owner (like living in your home after the trust owns it) nullifying the trust and those assets reverting to the estate. If you go this route, do it carefully to make sure it's created and maintained properly.

Living outside of Canada and the US

You can be a tax resident of the US and Canada while living in a third country, requiring you to file taxes in all three countries. In order to avoid this scenario while living abroad, you'd need to prove to the CRA that you've permanently severed your ties to Canada and/or renounce your US citizenship. However, that seems like a drastic action to take to avoid filing a few papers once a year.

Just as you don't pay double taxes while living in Canada, you won't owe triple taxes while living in a third country. Canada allows you to report exempt foreign income on line 256. Remember that different types of income, even from the same country, are taxed differently.

You'll need to check with the pertinent tax treaty to see what foreign income is exempt. While you won't owe taxes on this income, you'll still need to report it.

Reporting foreign taxes paid to a third country is the same as reporting taxes you've paid to the US. Report foreign federal taxes paid on T2209. Report foreign provincial/state and local taxes paid on T2036. Each country you paid more than C$200 in taxes to requires its own form. The amount from these forms goes on line 405 of your Schedule 1. This will provide tax credits to offset any taxes you might otherwise owe in Canada.

Previously, there was the Overseas Employment Tax Credit (OETC). Unlike the US foreign income tax exclusion, the OETC doesn't require that you establish residency in another country. The OETC allowed you to exclude 80% of your foreign income, up to $80k. The OETC was phased out and ended in 2016.

Canadian exit tax

When I first heard about the exit tax I had a moment of panic. It sounded like I would owe taxes on all of my property, as if I'd sold it at fair market value, if I ever stopped being a Canadian resident. What if I needed to move back to the US for a year or two when my parents are older?!

There's no need to panic, nor do you need an accountant to save you

from financial ruin.
    If you're panicking, here's the gist of it:
- If you've been a resident for fewer than 60 months in the last 10 years this doesn't apply
- This only applies if you are planning on leaving Canada permanently
- You have to tell the CRA about all of your assets, but you probably won't owe anything
- This isn't an additional tax, it's just paying capital gains taxes in two parts and adjusting your cost basis accordingly
- Most of us have all or the majority of our net worth in assets that are exempt from capital gains taxes (like your home and retirement accounts)
- If you do owe any capital gains taxes, you can defer payment until you actually sell

The Canadian exit tax is very similar to how US citizens are taxed upon renouncing their citizenship. Once you've paid the exit tax, you don't have to file taxes in Canada anymore, unless you have Canadian sourced income.

Who does the exit tax apply to?

Anyone who is a Canadian resident for more than five years has to navigate the exit tax, or deemed disposition rule. This is for both citizens and residents.

You can avoid the tax if you move out of Canada any time within the first 60 months of residency. However, to do this you would need to terminate your resident permit or give up your permanent resident status.

If your move to Canada is short-term, you'll want to plan to be there for less than 60 months within ten years if you have significant assets that will be taxed under the deemed disposition rules.

You only fall under the deemed disposition rules if you are leaving Canada for good. If your move is only temporary (even if you stay abroad for several years) you don't have to pay the exit tax. I can return to my hometown to take care of my parents in their old age without worrying about the exit tax. However, I'll still need to file taxes in Canada while I'm living outside of the country as long as I plan on coming back, because I'll be a factual resident of Canada for tax purposes.

People make a big fuss about how the US is the only country that taxes citizens living abroad on their worldwide income, but that's nonsense. Canada does the same thing.

In order to owe the exit tax you have to prove to the CRA that you've severed your ties to Canada and are moving permanently. The CRA isn't just going to spring this on you. In fact, if you haven't sold your home in Canada they might reject your claim. You'll also need to bring your spouse and dependents with you, if you have them, or provide a good reason for them to not come with you. Taking a look at form NR73 will show you the factors the CRA considers when deciding if you are no longer a Canadian tax resident.

While the exit tax seems punitive at first glance, it makes sense. When you do eventually sell these assets, you'll owe Canadian taxes on the sale. However, once you've left the country and have no plans to return, it will be much more difficult to ensure you actually pay. This way, Canada makes sure you can't leave the country and avoid paying your fair share.

What gets taxed?

When you apply to end your residency in Canada, the CRA requires you to report on your worldwide accounts on T1135: Foreign Income Verification Statement. Assets and accounts can't be sheltered from the tax just because they're abroad.

Your retirement accounts and any other tax-sheltered account are not taxed under deemed disposition rules, so your 401k, 403b, IRA, pension, RRSP, RESP, TFSA, and similar accounts are safe. Any trusts are also exempt, because a trust is a separate legal entity from you personally, so it's not moving with you.

Canadian real estate is exempt from the exit tax, since it's not like you can avoid paying taxes on that when you do sell.

Your Canadian real estate

If you sell your primary residence before you leave or soon after, you won't owe taxes on any capital gains. Sales after you become a non-resident will be subject to a 25% withholding, which you can have returned once you've filed T2062 and the CRA provides a certificate of compliance.

If you rent it at market rate, ideally to someone who isn't a family member, owning a home in Canada won't count as a residential tie. Once it becomes a rental property, your home will be subject to non-exempt capital gains for any amount of time it's rented out, as per change in use rules.

If you keep your home in Canada, perhaps using it as a vacation home, the CRA may not view you as a non-resident. Leaving your home in Canada vacant or allowing family members to live there for less than market rate may lead them to decide you are still a tax resident of Canada.

Your former home in Canada cannot be considered your principal residence for years you are not a tax resident of Canada. Capital gains from prior years will still be tax exempt, so you'll want to get the property assessed to update the cost basis.

If you have a rental property in Canada, you will need to report this income by filing a Canadian tax return, even if your deductions eliminate your tax liabilities.

Are you really paying extra taxes?

Many people have their net worth as a small amount of money for emergencies in savings, with most of their savings in retirement accounts, and their home. They probably also have a car and some personal items. They wouldn't owe exit taxes on any of this. Cars and other personal items rarely appreciate over time, so you're probably not going to owe capital gains. Your home and tax-sheltered accounts are exempt.

Let's be honest: if you are really leaving Canada forever, aren't you probably going to be moving your money to your new country? Anything you sell is only going to be taxed once, either from the actual sale or the theoretical sale (ie. the deemed disposition).

Any assets you don't sell will acquire a new cost basis from the date you pay the exit tax, so you won't be double taxed in Canada when you do eventually sell. Essentially, you owe the same amount of capital gains, you just pay it in two parts.

If you sell foreign assets you paid a Canadian exit tax for while you're a tax resident of the US, Article XIII(7) of the Canada-US Tax Convention prevents you from paying capital gains taxes twice on the same sale. This adjusts the cost basis to its value at the time of your emigration from Canada.

Minimizing capital gains taxes

There's a lot of advice out there suggesting spouses transfer high-value assets to the spouse with a lower income in order to reduce the amount of capital gains tax owed. This is tricky, since attribution rules require that the high-income spouse gives up their Canadian residency before the low-income spouse in order for this trick to work.

The CRA can easily argue that the high-income spouse is still a resident until their low-income spouse also leaves the country, since both retain significant ties to Canada.

Don't attempt tax evasion. There are ways to minimize capital gains taxes that don't require tricky moves or legal grey areas. Remember, taxes fund everything that keeps the country running, which is a good thing to contribute your part toward.

Declaring yourself a non-resident

You'll want to update your address with the CRA as soon as you move. The year you leave Canada forever, you'll need to file your taxes a little differently. This will feel familiar from when you filed taxes as a US domiciled resident for the last time.

Declare your worldwide income, as usual, for the period of the year when you were a Canadian resident. From the date you stopped being a resident, only declare your income from Canadian sources.

You'll need to file form NR73 and convince the CRA that you no longer live in Canada. This involves demonstrating that you have left Canada permanently. To do this, you'll need to do things like:
- Sell your home or rent it out on a long-term lease
- Move all of your things out of the country (don't leave them in storage in Canada)
- Establish a new home outside of Canada (aka buy or rent a home)
- Be required to pay taxes in another country (and be ready to prove this)
- Get a job with a non-Canadian company or get transferred to a foreign office
- Get a new driver's license in another country
- Give up your Canadian work permit, study permit, or permanent resident status
- Get new health insurance coverage
- Have a reason for any Canadian bank accounts you're keeping open
- Resign from your Canadian professional organizations or unions
- Join new community groups abroad

If you have more than C$25k, excluding your home, cash, retirement savings, and personal use property, you'll need to file T1161 and list your worldwide assets.

Do you have to pay right away?

Even if you owe money for the exit tax, you don't need to pay immediately. This tax is designed to prevent tax evasion by non-residents, not to punish people for leaving.

You calculate your deemed disposition of property on T1243. You can also file T1244 with your final tax return as a resident, requesting that you not pay any taxes on the deemed disposition until you actually sell the assets.

The CRA may require that you provide adequate security if you owe over C$100k in capital gains tax. That's not the value of the asset, it's the amount you'd owe on taxes on your profit, so this only applies to people with an extremely high net worth. No interest is charged on the deferred tax.

Other requirements for new non-residents

The RRSP Home Buyer's Plan will need to be paid within 60 days of your departure or this will be taxable. Those 60 days will expire before you file taxes for the year, so stay on top of this if it applies to you.

While you can keep your RRSP and TFSA, you will no longer receive annual contribution room so you can't make any additional contributions. If you want to add to these, you'll need to max them out before you leave.

If you keep accounts open in Canada, let your bank and investment firm know you're no longer a Canadian resident. They'll start automatically collecting taxes on your accounts and issuing you an NR4 instead of a T3 or T5.

You'll lose your provincial health coverage and need to re-apply if you ever return.

What happens if you don't pay the exit tax?

Once you've been a resident of Canada for more than 60 months, you're considered a tax resident of Canada until you pay the exit tax. You will need to file taxes in Canada annually. If you simply move and stop paying Canadian taxes; the CRA can freeze your Canadian accounts or put a lien on your assets.

If you stop filing taxes in Canada and the CRA doesn't notice, you'll still face issues if you ever return to Canada. This will mess up your GST/HST rebate and things like the Canada Child Benefit and Old Age Pension.

Reporting requirements as a non-resident

Once you declare to the CRA that you are no longer a Canadian resident, you'll be subject to non-resident withholding taxes on your Canadian income. You'll need to file a Canadian tax return and (potentially) pay taxes any year you have Canadian sourced income or capital gains. This is done by filing the Income Tax and Benefit Return for Non-Residents and Deemed Residents of Canada.

You don't need to file if your only Canadian income is from passive income that's already being reported on an NR4, such as dividends or interest. This is why it's important to let your bank and investment firm know you're no longer a resident, so they will withhold taxes for you. You'll be able to claim any taxes you pay as a foreign tax credit on your US return.

If you have reportable property valued at over C$25k, you'll need to report it annually on T1161. Cash, pension plans, retirement plans, and personal-use property valued at under C$10k is exempt.

Returning to Canada after the exit tax

If you move back to Canada, the day you become a Canadian resident establishes a new adjusted cost base for your property.

You can elect to unwind the deemed disposition, if you paid the exit tax. This could provide you with a refund on your unrealized capital gains. This could be beneficial if your marginal tax rate will be lower when you plan on selling the property than it was when you paid the deemed disposition tax. If you left Canada when you were earning a lot of money and moved back to Canada after retirement, this may work in your favor.

If you've deferred the exit tax and provided security, that security will be returned.

There is not a form for making this election. You'll have to write a letter to the CRA on or before the tax filing date of the year you re-establish Canadian tax residency. You'll be requesting an election under section 128.1(6)(c) of the Income Tax Act regarding the property.

Relinquishing your US green card

If you are a permanent resident in the US, you may be tempted to give this up in order to avoid having to file taxes on your worldwide income.

You can relinquish and then reacquire PR status in the US.

You'll need to file form I-407 with a US consular or immigration officer and they will determine that you have abandoned your status as a lawful permanent resident.

Renouncing US citizenship

Relinquishing your US citizenship by performing an expatriating act with the intention of relinquishing citizenship may get you in trouble at the border, but it has no bearing on your tax residency.

You need to appear before a diplomatic or consular officer outside of the US in order to renounce your citizenship. Some embassies require you to be a resident of the country in which the renunciation takes place.

Even if you can book an appointment online, you'll want to call and let them know that the appointment is for a US citizenship renunciation. You'll need to complete form DS-4079, 4080, and 4081 prior to your appointment.

There are actually two appointments: one to ensure you understand the implications of your actions. The second appointment gives you the opportunity to take an oath renouncing your citizenship.

During your appointment, you'll complete a number of papers, including DS-4082 and 4083. You also need to file form 8854 with the IRS. You'll need to pay a renunciation fee of $2,350.

Some embassies will confiscate your US passport at this point, as you are no longer a US citizen.

Once this is complete, you'll still need to wait several months to receive your Certificate of Loss of Nationality.

If the Department of Homeland Security determines that your renunciation was for the purpose of tax avoidance, you may be deemed inadmissible to the US under the Reed Amendment.

Renunciation does not prevent another country from deporting you to the US or prevent extradition. Entering the US with a foreign passport showing a US birthplace may lead to additional questions at the border.

Expatriating acts

You can backdate your relinquishing of citizenship if you can prove that you committed an expatriating act before 2004. This generally requires committing an act of treason or enlisting in the military of forces at war with the US.

If you moved to Canada to avoid the US military draft and assumed that becoming a Canadian citizen involved relinquishing your US citizenship, you may want to consult an attorney about this option.

Expatriation taxes and fees

Remember that you will need to file taxes for the year you renounce your citizenship, since you are still a tax resident until the day you renounce. This is done by filing a dual status return. You'll file a 1040 for the portion of the year you're a US tax resident and a 1040NR for after you ceased to be a resident.

You will still owe any back taxes. If the amount is considerable, they will not allow you to renounce your citizenship until you're in compliance with the IRS.

If you:
- have a net worth greater than $2 million USD on the day you renounce,
- have had an average federal tax liability of $160k or more per year in the past five years, or
- cannot certify tax compliance,

you need to pay taxes on your assets. There are some exceptions to this, such as people who became dual citizens at birth and lived in the US for fewer than 10 of the previous 15 years.

Your first $700k in assets are exempt from capital gains tax. You can use your gift allowance, including your lifetime gift allowance, to legally reduce the amount of your taxable net worth.

Be sure to research the tax implications this will have on your estate taxes and your ability to transfer assets between yourself and a spouse, if they are a US citizen.

You can still access Social Security and Medicare as a non-citizen. You will, however, forfeit military benefits and government pensions.

Renouncing your US citizenship is irrevocable and cannot be reversed.

Part Three: Canadian taxes

Filing Canadian taxes for the first time

If you're a newcomer, you might be nervous about filing taxes in Canada for the first time. Don't be. You'll likely find it simpler than filing with the IRS.

Just like filing US taxes, the amount of money you need to pay each year depends on how you file. You can allocate deductions among family members and make financial decisions in ways that legally reduce the amount of taxes you owe. Knowing the marginal tax rate (MTR) of different investment options can help maximize your assets over time. The better you understand tax laws, the better you can make smart financial decisions.

In Canada, you start with Schedule 1 for federal taxes and form 428 for your province or territory. Like the 1040 in the US, everyone has to complete this form and some people need additional forms, based on their specific tax situation.

The easiest way to file your taxes is by using tax software. Be sure to use software that covers your province and your specific situation. If you have foreign income or it's your first year in Canada, it's imperative that you select tax software that calculates your foreign tax credit.

The CRA encourages you to file your taxes online. You can even auto-fill your return with information submitted to the CRA.

In order to file online, you'll first need to create a myCRA account. You'll need to confirm your identity, create a username and password (or use your bank credentials), and provide the security code they'll send you in the mail. Because they send you a code through the postal system, you'll need to wait a few days to finalize your myCRA account setup. Once this is set up, you can opt to get your mail from the CRA electronically, although they may still sometimes send you things through the postal system.

The regular tax filing deadline is April 30th. If you are self-employed, the filing deadline is June 15th. However, all taxes are due on April 30th, so if you expect to owe taxes you should submit an estimated payment before April 30th.

In Canada you only have to file a single income tax return, since the federal government collects taxes on behalf of the provinces and territories. Except Quebec. As you know already, things are different in Quebec.

To get a quick idea of your allowable deductions and credits, take a look at the CRA's tax bracket thresholds and benefit amounts.

Things to do when you first arrive in Canada

After you get a SIN, you should apply for benefits and credits you're entitled to, like the GST/HST credit, provincial and territorial benefits and credits, and the Canada child benefit. If you're a permanent resident or a protected person, you're eligible to apply as soon as you land. If you're a temporary resident, you're eligible in your 19th month of living in Canada. You'll want to file:
- RC151 GST/HST credit application
- RC66 Canada child benefits application & RC66SCH Status in Canada
- Once you've filed for those benefits, you just have to file your income tax return and keep your personal information up to date.

Your tax forms will ask for your date of entry into Canada. This isn't necessarily the date you declared landing in Canada, this is when you became a Canadian resident for income tax purposes.

Personal details

Just like with a W-4 in the US, you'll need to file a TD1 at the start of a new job and update it if your life circumstances change. If you qualify for a large number of tax refunds, you can submit form T1213 to the CRA, who will notify your employer to reduce your tax withholdings.

If your income is commission based, you can use form TD1X to reduce your withholdings based on your expenses. You file this directly with your employer.

If you move, you'll need to submit a change of address. You're taxed based on the province or territory you live in on December 31st of the tax year.

You can file taxes for your children. This is beneficial if they have any amount of income or if they're 18 or older.

Marital status

Common-law couples are treated the same way as married couples. If your marital status changes, you need to file form RC 65 by the end of the month after the change. In case of separation, you must wait 90 days to file the form. If you divorce, some tax credits will be split and others will go to one person or the other.

If you are married or have dependents over 18, be sure to choose tax software that automatically links your tax returns together and allows you to optimize your allocation of deductions and credits. So long as it's legally possible, you'll want to allocate income and expenses to keep each spouse in the lowest tax bracket.

Breakdown	Percentage	Total income
First $45k is taxed at	15%	$45k
Next $45k is taxed at	20.5%	$90k
Next $50k is taxed at	26%	$140k
Next $60k is taxed at	29%	$200
Any income over $200k	33%	Over $200k

There are some instances where you can legally split your income between spouses or transfer assets to your spouse and children. Spouses can split their Canada Pension Plan and private pensions. Spouses can also transfer capital properties on a tax-free basis.

Just be careful of attribution rules whenever transferring money or assets to your spouse or children.

Attribution rules generally mean that whoever provided the initial cash is responsible for the income taxes, meaning they can be stuck paying taxes on gifts to spouses and children. This is meant to deter tax avoidance schemes.

Generally, attribution rules don't apply to funds invested in a TFSA, principal residence, education costs, car purchases, a child's or spouse's business, or other similar investments. Payments into a child's RRSP, RESP, or RDSP are also safe. If you loan money to a family member and charge interest, future profits are exempt from attribution rules.

If you're married or in a common-law relationship, you'll need to include their worldwide income on your tax return, even if they aren't a resident of Canada.

RRSP & PRPP

Your earned income will be used to calculate your RRSP or PRPP contribution allowance. Like a traditional IRA, an RRSP can reduce your taxable income in both the US and Canada. You won't be assigned an RRSP contribution amount until you've filed taxes in Canada for the first time.

Your employer can make PRPP contributions on your behalf, but you can't deduct that portion on your tax return. Those contributions aren't considered employment income, however, and aren't taxed. Employer contributions are reported on line 205 of your income tax return.

When you make a withdrawl from your PRPP you will have to report this as income. This may impact the amount you receive from OAS and GIS, which are determined based on your income.

Policies

You'll want to retain tax records for six years. Generally, electronic copies are acceptable.

You can amend a tax return for up to ten years after it was due.

A simple income tax return

If you live alone, have been a Canadian resident for the whole year, and have a single salary from a Canadian company, filing your taxes will be a breeze.

Enter your personal information. The CRA computes your GST/HST credits. Enter your T4 and any other T slips, if they haven't autocompleted. You're done!

A complex income tax return

Many of us have more than a single T4 to report. Here's guidance on what to pay attention to when filing your Canadian taxes as a newcomer.

Reporting your income

All income you earned in the tax year must be reported. Different income is reported in different ways and is taxed separately.

Residency

If you were only a resident of Canada for part of the year, you still have to report some income from the part of the year you weren't a Canadian resident. When you weren't a resident, you still have to declare income from a Canadian source, including salaries, capital gains, and any taxable scholarships, fellowships, etc. If the money came from Canada, you need to report it to Canada.

There's one exception to this rule: if the Canadian-sourced income was taxed in your home country and it's exempt from taxation through a tax treaty, you may not have to report it. Check the rules carefully.

For the part of the year you were a resident, you have to report your worldwide income. Even if it's exempt from taxes thanks to a tax treaty, you have to report it. You then deduct the tax exempt portion on line 256.

Foreign income

If you work for a foreign company, you have to report this income on your Canadian tax return. Be sure to convert all amounts into Canadian dollars before you report it. Some tax software does this automatically, so be careful to make sure the numbers are correct.

If the income is not taxable in Canada because of a tax treaty, you deduct it from line 256. If it is taxable in Canada, you complete form T2209 and claim a foreign tax credit on line 405. Most tax software will calculate the foreign tax credit for you.

Salaries and wages

If you work for a Canadian company as an employee, you fill out the TD1 when you start and you'll get a T4 outlining your salary and/or wages at the end of the year. You can enter multiple T4s if you've had more than one job.

If you lose a T4, you can login to your CRA account and view the T4 the company submitted to the CRA. If you don't receive a T4 and there's no form submitted with the CRA, you can use your pay stubs to estimate your earnings and deductions. You can also reach out to your HR department to get a copy from them.

If there's an error on your T4, you'll need to get the company to correct it. Don't just adjust the numbers on your own. If they refuse to make a correction, include a letter to the CRA explaining the situation when you file.

If you got another T4 after you submitted your tax return, you can amend your return with a T1-ADJ. This can't be filed online, so you'll have to mail it in.

Some job benefits are taxable. Others are not. Check to make sure you're paying taxes on what you owe and not overpaying.

Taxable benefits include:
- Board and lodging or discounted rent
- Personal use of a company car
- Cash gifts (depending on amount) as well as prizes or awards (over $500)
- Provincial health and hospital premiums, other insurance plans
- Gains and income on stock options

Tax free benefits include:
- Travel expenses, meals and travel for overtime
- Travel passes for employees (but not their families)
- Social and athletic club memberships
- Tuition for courses required by your employer
- Moving expenses for your job
- Employee counseling for health, retirement, and re-employment
- Private health plan premiums
- Wage loss replacement plan payments
- Attendants for disabled employees

Rental income

Rental income is reported on form T776 and lines 126 to 160. If you're renting out a property at below fair market value, you could be setting yourself up for an audit and additional taxes, especially if you're renting to a relative.

If you own the rental property with your spouse or someone else, rental income is subject to attribution rules. Whoever provided the capital to acquire the property is responsible for the income taxes. If both owners provided capital, they are each responsible for a share of the income respective to the initial capital they provided. Money in joint accounts is handled the same way.

You can deduct rental expenses like mortgage interest, utilities, property taxes, condo/HOA fees, insurance, landscaping, advertising, legal fees, office supplies, and maintenance costs. You can deduct the cost of renovations you made to make the property accessible (as opposed to treating them as a capital improvement). Be sure to classify capital improvements and claim depreciation, called capital cost allowance, properly. In Canada claiming depreciation is optional.

Remember that land doesn't depreciate in value, so you need to separate the cost of the land and only claim depreciation on improvements. Your property tax assessment will break down these values for you. If you claim depreciation on a rental property that's part of your primary residence, you may be putting your future capital gains exemption at risk or complicating your future reporting. Claiming depreciation is not mandatory, so you may not want to claim depreciation on appreciating assets to avoid having to pay it back when you sell.

If you sell investment properties, it can be considered income or capital gain, depending on whether your real estate investing is a business. This is generally only a consideration if you continually flip houses or own a property purely for the capital increase.

Capital gains

Investment income will be reported to you on a T3 or T5. If you have foreign investment income, be sure to claim any applicable foreign tax credits and convert all amounts into Canadian dollars.

Remember that interest paid on money you borrowed to invest is deductible. You can also deduct investment counseling costs.

When calculating capital gains on the sale of any property you brought with you to Canada when you immigrated, the fair market value on the day you landed is used as the base cost. This is deemed acquisition. You declared the fair market value of all of your possessions on your B4 when you landed in Canada.

Plenty of people get settled in Canada before they become Canadian residents, so there's an exception to this rule. If you purchased real estate in Canada prior to your immigration or acquired capital within Canada, you can use the original purchase price as the base cost.

Canada has a lifetime capital gains tax exemption of approximately $866.9k, tied to inflation, but only for qualifying properties. These include small business corporation shares, farm property, and fishing properties.

Capital gains from your primary residence are not taxed in Canada. Each household can only claim a single primary residence per year. If a home was a primary residence for only part of the time you owned it, you may need to pay capital gains on a portion of the proceeds. If you sold your former primary residence shortly after you became a Canadian resident, you will not owe taxes on the sale.

If you own a home but decide to rent it out, you can keep the property for up to four years and still claim the capital gains tax exemption. If you relocate for work and remain with that employer or move back into the home by the end of the calendar year when you leave their employ, you can avoid any capital gains taxes on the eventual sale, even if you stay longer than four years.

Unincorporated home businesses

Personal business or partnership income is reported on form T2125 and on lines 135 to 143. You're responsible to self report your net income (after deductions) on your personal tax return.

Businesses in farming and fishing, as well as those taking part in the AgriInvest program, have separate reporting requirements.

It goes without saying that you have to keep proper accounting records. Cash businesses with unreported income are tax evasion. If you've been operating a cash business, you can participate in the voluntary disclosures program and sort things out with the CRA.

Partnership income is divided among the partners based on the partnership agreement. The CRA recognizes that partners invest more than just cash into the agreement — they also bring labour, property, and skills. If one member of the partnership has another full-time job and the other is dedicated to the partnership full-time, it's understandable that the split might not be 50/50. You'll have specific reporting requirements if your business has significant assets.

Remember that small businesses may be required to collect GST and/or HST. If you have gross revenue under $30k and provide less than $30k in supplies per quarter, you may not need to collect GST/HST. Check tax requirements carefully. If you have a business that collects GST/HST and has employees, you'll need to file income returns and make payments.

Bartered goods must be reported as income according to their fair market value.

Deductible expenses must be divided according to operational and capital status. Operating expenses include rent, office supplies, professional fees, travel expenses, wages, printing, shipping, advertising, insurance, and utilities. Capital assets are depreciated. Deductible expenses in the US and Canada are pretty similar, but not the same. By keeping these differences in mind as you record your expenses during the year you can save yourself some time when you do your taxes.

You can use losses in your home business to offset other income. Losses can be applied to three previous years and forward up to 20 years. The ability to carry forward startup costs to offset other income is a common reason to put off incorporating. Family businesses are often a legal way to split income and reduce the amount of taxes you owe. Of course, the work must actually be done, the pay must be reasonable, and all employment laws need to be followed.

If your home business is your primary source of income or your side business is particularly successful, you'll have to make CPP contributions. This is calculated on your schedule 8.

In addition to keeping records of your income and expenses, a written business plan can go a long way toward faring well if you get audited. You'll need to demonstrate that the goal of your business is to make an income (eventually) and that it is not a hobby.

Retirement income

Your CPP, QPP, and OAS are all reported on lines 113 and 114.

Other income

You are required to self-report tips and gratuities. The CRA has been known to check restaurant records, where tips are recorded for all debit and credit card transactions.

If you have a research grant, you are allowed to subtract reasonable expenses related to your research and report only the net income. You cannot, however, report a loss if you spent more than the amount of your grant.

Unemployment insurance (EI) is taxable in most instances.

If you're a protected person and have received funds or support from a charitable organization, like a church group or nonprofit, you don't have to report this as income. If a charitable organization hired you to do work, you'll need to report it as employment income.

Be sure to report all of your worldwide income. If there is not a specific line to report a type of income, it goes on line 130, other income. This includes annuity payments, death benefits, pension plan lump-sum payments, severance pay, RESP payments, training allowances, and trust payments.

Non-taxable income

Not all income is taxed in Canada. Exempt income includes:
- TFSA earnings and withdrawals
- Inheritance and gifts
- Life insurance policy proceeds
- Lottery winnings
- Foster care payments
- Canadian Forces in high-risk international mission income
- Provincial and federal refundable tax credits, child tax benefits
- Canadian service pensions, war veterans allowance, and compensation for holocaust survivors, military disability pensions, RCMP disability pension and compensation
- Proceeds from accident, disability, illness, or income maintenance plans
- Income exempt by statute

If you have income outside of wages and freelance income, check to see if it's taxable.

Tax credits

As in the US, there are two types of tax credits: refundable and nonrefundable credits. If you have refundable credits, you can get a tax return even without having had taxes withheld from your income. With nonrefundable credits, you can reduce your taxes owed to zero.

Most tax credits in Canada are indexed to inflation, so they increase each year.

Most tax software will calculate your federal refundable tax credits, provincial refundable tax credits, off the tax return, and non-refundable tax credits for you.

Many tax credits are calculated automatically. These include:
- GST/HST credit
- Anyone with employment income can claim the Canada employment amount. This is meant to cushion the cost of your commute, normal work clothes, and other incidentals.
- Amount for children under 18
- Pension income amount
- Universal child care benefit (UCCB)
- UCCB bonus for single parents
- Canada child tax benefit (CCTB)
- The family caregiver amount (FCA) increases the tax credits for the spousal amount, amount for eligible dependent, amount for children under 19, and the caregiver amount.
- The disability amount and the disability amount for children.
- If your spouse is 65+, you can claim the age amount.

Other common credits:
- Medical expense credits are reduced by 3% of your net income, so the spouse with a lower income should claim them. Private health insurance and travel insurance premiums can be deducted.
- The cost of moving to a new home to accommodate a newly disabled spouse can trigger a tax credit. You can also write off part of the cost of a van for a disabled family member.
- Working income tax benefit (WITB)
- Children's fitness amount for eligible sports and fitness expenses for children under 16.
- Children's arts amount is for artistic, cultural, recreational, or developmental activities.
- Home buyer tax credit
- Student loan interest tax credit

- Tuition, education, and textbook tax credit for post-secondary education.
- The charitable contribution tax credit should be claimed on one return to maximize the credit. In 2016 and 2017, if you haven't made a prior claim for the donation credit (since 2007) you can apply an additional 25% credit for cash donations up to $1k. You can carry claims forward for five years. Political contributions are also deductible.
- Adoption expenses

Often, if one spouse doesn't have a high enough income to claim a tax credit, it will be transferred to the other spouse. Otherwise, it will automatically be assigned to the lower-earning spouse.

Common deductions

There are numerous expenses you can deduct from your taxes. There are special deductions for Canadian Armed Forces personnel, police officers, transport employees, and northern residents. While I've outlined the most common deductions, check with the CRA to make sure you're not overpaying.

Deduct your RRSP contributions or report an overpayment on your schedule 8 and line 208. If you've never filed taxes in Canada before, you can't claim this RRSP deduction but you can claim the deduction the second year you file taxes in Canada. You're allowed an over-contribution of $2k over the course of your life. Any over contribution over that amount is subject to penalties.

The disability supports deduction is for expenses that allow a disabled person to go to work, conduct research, or study at a post-secondary school. This is taken on line 219.

Employee stock options get special treatment on line 249.

Line 221 is for carrying charges, including safe deposit boxes and investment loans.

Child care expenses

The cost of childcare is claimed on form T778 and line 214. You can claim babysitting, daycare, a live-in nanny, and types of lodging (for boarding schools, day camps, and overnight camps). You cannot claim medical care, clothing, transportation, or tuition. Only one parent may claim this deduction. Typically it's the supporting parent with the lowest income, unless the lower-earner was a student or incapable of providing child care.

Remember that you'll need receipts if you're audited. You can't claim payments to anyone you claim as a dependent, such as paying one child to watch another or paying an elderly parent you support.

If you make child support payments you can deduct these, regardless of where the other parent lives.

Moving expenses

Sadly, you usually can't deduct the cost of moving to Canada. There's an exception if you're a full-time student with taxable income, or if you're a factual or deemed resident moving back to Canada.

Moving expenses from one Canadian home to another Canadian home can be claimed if you got a new job, are moving closer to work or school, or to run a business at a new location. Obviously, you can't deduct any expenses you were reimbursed for. These are reported on form T1-M and line 219.

In order to deduct moving expenses, you must have earned income in that calendar year related to the job you moved for. You can carry over moving expenses to apply against income in the next year. Full-time students (or co-op students) can claim against research grants, awards, summer jobs, and employment income.

Moving expenses include the cost of selling your old home, carrying costs of a vacant residence, purchasing the new home, traveling to your new home, storage and moving costs, and temporary living expenses.

You can't claim a loss on your old home or deduct improvements you made to sell your old home. House hunting and job hunting expenses aren't eligible. Neither are the value of things you couldn't move, cleaning expenses, replacement costs, mail forwarding, plug adapters and transformers, or GST on your home purchase.

If your employer requires you to move and offers you a low-interest or interest free home loan, you must pay taxes on this benefit. You can note it on line 248.

Employment expenses

In order to claim employment expenses, you'll need to get your employer to sign form T2200. You don't need to file T2200, but you'll want it on hand in case you're audited. You'll detail expenses on form T777 (which must be submitted) and declare them on line 229 of your tax return.

For complete information about allowable employment expenses, read T4044.

If you're a salaried employee, you can deduct travel expenses (including meals, tips, and lodging), parking and vehicle expenses (but not for commuting), office supplies, and salaries for an assistant (including paying a spouse or dependent to do this work).

If you earn commission, you can deduct additional travel and sales expenses, including promotions, entertainment, and home office costs.

Expenses may only be applied to income in the calendar year, so beware of spending large sums of money in hopes of future earnings.

Capital expenditures, like a cell phone or computer aren't deductible for employers if they're purchased outright. They can, however, be deducted if they're leased, which might make it worthwhile to lease a phone instead of buying one. The rules for equipment purchases are very specific, so check with the CRA before you sign a contract.

The CRA is very nitpicky about cell phone plans being deducted as a business expense. They love to disavow cell phone plans, especially data, even if you only deduct a portion of your plan. If you're audited they'll want to see a breakdown of the usage for your plan to show that it really is being used for business. It sounds like an impossible task, but substantiating that my cell phone plan is mostly for business only took a few minutes. Because so many of my friends use WhatsApp, the only phone calls and nearly all the texts that showed up in my phone company usage report were my parents, my boss, and other work calls. It was very easy to demonstrate my call/text history breakdown in a spreadsheet with a little sorting. The vast majority of my data usage corresponded with business trips (why is conference center and airport wifi so bad?!) so in the end they allowed me to keep the deduction. Be prepared to back up your deduction with data.

There are specific rules for artists and musicians, forestry workers, apprentice vehicle mechanics, and tradespersons.

You may be eligible for GST/HST rebates on employment expenses using form GST370.

Home office expenses are a common reason for an audit, so be sure to keep all related documents and receipts. When I was audited I was asked to provide floor plans and photos demonstrating what portion of my home was used as a home office and to show that it really was a dedicated office space.

Salaried employees can claim rent, utilities, maintenance (including cleaning supplies), and repairs for a home office or rented office space. Commissioned employees can also claim insurance and property taxes. Self employed people can also claim a capital cost allowance (CCA). Claiming a CCA can impact your principal residence exemption.

Your home office expenses are limited to the amount of related income, so you can't claim a loss.

You can deduct union dues, professional board dues, and professional insurance premiums.

Foreign assets and income

If you have more than $100k in assets abroad, like in the US, at any point during the year, you'll need to file form T1135. Not all assets need to be reported, including:
- Vacation homes
- Business property
- Property in a retirement or pension plan
- Mutual funds
- Shares in a foreign affiliate

Generally, if your foreign asset is for your exclusive personal use, it doesn't have to be reported. Check with the CRA to see what you need to report.

If this is your first Canadian tax return since you immigrated, you don't have to file this form. If you still have $100k in assets abroad the second time you file taxes, you'll have to report them.

After you file

Shortly after you've submitted your Canadian tax return, you'll get a notice of assessment from the CRA. This will outline what they believe you owe or are owed. If there's a discrepancy between your numbers and the numbers the CRA calculated, you can ask them for more information and file a notice of objection.

You have 90 days to file a notice of objection with form T400A. Some people opt to mail a letter instead.

Making a payment

If you owe taxes, you can make a payment to the CRA by online bank transfer, debit card, credit card, wire transfer, by mail, or in person at a service center or many banks.

Filing for a refund

If you have paid more in taxes than you owe or you qualify for refundable tax credits, you can get your refund through direct deposit. If you don't provide direct deposit information they'll mail a cheque to the address the CRA has on file.

CRA audits

Every year the CRA audits tax filings that seem likely to contain errors or have indications of possible non-compliance.

If you're chosen for an audit, the CRA will ask you to send them copies of your records. You can mail copies of your documents to the CRA, but they would prefer you upload documents through your myCRA account. The letter they provide you with will include information on what documents they would like to review and give you a deadline to submit them. They're pretty flexible and will typically review documents submitted after the deadline.

They may also provide you with a time for an in-person meeting, likely at your home or accountant's office.

The CRA can request documents not only from you, but also from family members, trusts, and associated businesses. The letter advising you that you're being audited will outline what records they are asking for.

The audit may entail matching up your numbers on your tax returns to your business records. They may want to see that your spending, investments, and savings match up with your declared income.

If your records are incomplete, you'll have to track down the information to fill in what's missing. The better your record keeping, the easier the audit will be and the faster it will be over. Plus, good records minimize the likelihood that you'll have made an error in the first place!

Most audits catch honest mistakes or misinterpretations of tax laws. If this is the case, you'll have to adjust your filings and may owe money, but it's unlikely that you'll face penalties.

Part Four: US taxes

Getting caught up

If you've been living in Canada for a while and haven't filed your US taxes, the IRS knows. Since 2013, Canadian banks and investment firms have been asking if you're a US tax resident and providing the US with your information.

Back in 2011, the US had the Voluntary Offshore Disclosure Program, which made it easier for people to come clean about their foreign earnings and assets.

You probably haven't been using your foreign income and accounts as a tax shelter. Most people who are remiss in filing US taxes either didn't realize they had to or kept putting it off. Luckily, you're considered to be in compliance for any year that you wouldn't have owed US taxes. That's most of you, if you're living in Canada.

Generally, the IRS will only expect you to go back for the past six years. However, there has been at least one case where someone was held responsible for 30 years of back taxes.

If you've been filing taxes in Canada (or another country) you already have just about all of the information you need to run the math and catch up with your back taxes so you're in compliance.

While the IRS can pursue you for unpaid taxes for ten years, you can only file for a refund within three years from the tax filing due date.

Filing US tax forms for previous years

If you've been filing taxes in Canada, your Canadian return should have all of the information you need to file with the IRS. You can login to the CRA website to get personal income tax returns, information slips, and statement of income or deductions from previous years.

If you were working for a US employer, you can contact the IRS and request that they mail you a wage and income transcript. This will go back ten years and list all of the W-2 and 1099 information the IRS has on file.

Your employer (or former employer) can also provide you with tax documents for previous years.

Tax laws change each year, so you'll need to prepare taxes for each year on the correct forms. You can get old copies of tax forms on the IRS website. If you're using tax preparation software, make sure it's the right version for the year you're filing for.

You won't be able to submit old returns online, they need to be mailed in.

Penalties for overdue taxes

If you owe more than $10k in taxes and have bank accounts in the US, they'll likely be frozen until you settle up with the IRS. If you have any assets in the US, like real estate, they can issue a tax lien. This is a legal claim against your asset which appears if you attempt to sell a property and shows up on your credit report. If you sell the property, the IRS will get their cut first. If the property sells for less than what you owe in taxes, you'll still be responsible for paying the difference. They can also seize the property and sell it on your behalf.

Once you pay your tax debt the lien will be removed. If you set up a payment plan with the IRS, the lien will be removed after three consecutive payments. If the IRS fails to remove the lien automatically, you can file form 12277: Application for Withdrawal.

Tax penalty abatement

If you owe taxes, you can avoid penalties by showing reasonable cause for failing to have filed and paid on time with a first time penalty abatement waiver. You'll need to show reasonable cause for why you weren't able to file on time. You'll need to have caught up on your filing obligations in order to qualify.

Generally, reasonable cause is granted if you've faced a serious illness, a house fire, death of a spouse, or something of similar gravity. If you genuinely did not know you were obligated to file US taxes, you stand a shot. If your old accountant gave you bad advice, you can blame them, just be prepared to back up your claim with documents.

You can request penalty abatement over the phone, online, or in writing. The IRS can remove the penalty immediately or require that you first pay your outstanding tax debt. If they've agreed to waive the penalty once you've paid your taxes, all interest accrued on the penalty will also be waived.

You will still be required to pay interest on whatever amount you owe.

Offers in compromise

With an offer in compromise, the IRS will let you settle your tax debt for less than you actually owe. Generally, the IRS will accept an offer that represents what they expect they would be able to get you to pay if they attempted to collect the full debt. If you have a modest income and little savings, the IRS will likely accept a reasonable offer.

You have to be up to date with your tax filings in order to qualify. You also can't be in bankruptcy.

You can submit an offer in compromise for debuts of up to $100k. You can pay in one lump sum or several payments.

Setting up a tax debt payment plan

If you want to negotiate the amount owed, you need to do this before you set up a payment plan.

The IRS will allow you to set up an installation agreement to pay your tax debt over time. You can apply through form 9465: Installation Agreement Request or the IRS's online payment agreement tool as long as your tax debt is less than $50k, including interest and penalties. There are fees, ranging from $89 to $225, to set this up. There are lower rates available for people with low incomes.

If your debt is under $10k and the math on your monthly payments works out to paying it off in full in three years, the IRS will almost certainly accept the proposed installation payment.

You must pay whatever amount you propose each month, but you're free to pay more. Any future tax refunds will automatically be applied to your debt.

The IRS will respond to your proposal within 30 days. They will automatically reject your proposal if you haven't filed all of your outstanding tax returns.

Payments can be made by mail or through IRS Direct Pay. If you find yourself unable to make a payment, contact the IRS at 1-800-829-1040 as soon as you realize. They can help you adjust your payment schedule if you reach out. If you don't contact them, they'll send you to collections.

Currently not collectible debts

If you demonstrate to the IRS that you can't pay your tax debt without facing undue hardship, the IRS will stop trying to collect it. They'll review your tax returns every two years to see if your circumstances have changed. If they determine that you can now pay some or all of your debt, they'll contact you.

If your income is from social security, welfare, or unemployment or you are unemployed, they will give you a currently not collectible designation, or status 53. They may require significant documentation in form 433-F or 433-A, or they may not.

The goal of the IRS is not to bankrupt you. If paying your tax debt would mean you would not be able to pay your rent, keep your utilities on, cover healthcare expenses, stay in school, or be able to get to your job, they will work with you to reduce your debt or choose not to collect it.

Of course, if they feel your living expenses are lavish, they'll expect you to downsize your McMansion before they forgive your debt. The IRS has collection financial standards that outline what they consider reasonable necessary expenses. They will not give you a status 53 if you have access to savings or assets that could be sold to pay your debt.

Statute of limitations on collecting tax debt

The ten year statute of limitations on collecting taxes begins when the IRS determines you owe money, either at the conclusion of an audit or when you file your return. Any filing you add to that (for that year) restarts the clock on the statute of limitations. After the statute of limitations expires, any tax liens become unenforceable.

The IRS can freeze your US bank accounts, put a lien on your US property, or even pursue criminal prosecution. However, this is unlikely. In most cases, you'll simply be required to pay a penalty based on how much you owe.

The Simple 1040 scenario

If you earn a salary and make less than this year's foreign earned income exclusion (FEIE) and don't have any other income, your tax forms will be quite simple. This is assuming you live in Canada permanently (or have spent at least 330 days outside of the US this year).

Your Canadian employer will give you a T4. Convert this amount into USD and fill in line 7 of the 1040.

Use form 2555 or 2555-EZ to calculate your FEIE. You enter this as a negative number on line 21 on your 1040.

Assuming your FEIE is equal to or greater than your gross income, you have no taxable income.

You don't have to worry about other exclusions, deductions, taxes, and credits. You cannot claim both the FEIE and the earned income credit (EIC) if you have no taxable income.

Because your Canadian employer did not withhold any US taxes from your paycheck, you are not eligible for a US tax refund.

Yes, it feels a bit like you're submitting a blank 1040, but that's normal. Aren't you glad you didn't pay an accountant to do that?

More complex 1040 scenarios

Unfortunately, not all of us are so lucky when it comes to tax filing. If you're like me, your taxes are quite a bit more complex than a salary (or two) and standard deductions. Here's how to handle some common tax scenarios.

The Tax Cuts and Jobs Act has made significant changes to tax law for 2019. However, most of the changes are a moot point for Americans living abroad. If you're using tax software to prepare your taxes, it will incorporate changes in the tax brackets and reflect the switch from indexed amounts to Chained CPI.

The biggest consideration is guessing if your deductions will be greater than the $12.2k standard deduction. If they're not, it's not worth the hassle of itemizing and potentially substantiating deductions.

Income

Canada and the US have different ideas of what's taxable income on a W-2 or T4. If you're concerned about this, you can ask your employer for a breakdown and check with the IRS to see what's taxable and non-taxable income. This is probably not worth the hassle in most instances, but it may be if you make more than the FEIE and your job comes with considerable in-kind benefits that are taxable in Canada and not taxed in the US.

Interest and dividend income

You'll get a T5 and/or a 1099-INT to report any interest or dividend income you've earned. If you have more than $1,500 in interest and dividend income, you'll have to complete a Schedule B.

If you have a TFSA in Canada, you'll have to report the investment income to the US as you would with any other investment account.

You may have heard about the net investment income tax. This tax can't be eliminated with foreign tax credits, so people really don't like it. Luckily for us, it doesn't apply to people who are tax residents of another country.

Alimony

The IRS is changing how future alimony payments are taxed. If you're receiving alimony in an agreement reached on January 1, 2019 or after, alimony payments made can't be deducted from your taxable income and alimony payments received aren't considered taxable income.

If you have an existing agreement from 2018 or before, your tax situation for alimony remains the same.

Freelance income

As someone who does freelance work for US companies, it can occasionally take some wrangling to get them to issue me 1099s. Many bookkeepers fail to realize that US citizens are still US persons as far as the IRS is concerned, regardless of their residency status.

If a client doesn't issue you a 1099, you should calculate the amount and report it yourself.

Capital gains and losses

If you've sold a capital asset, you'll need to report the gain or loss to the IRS. The most common capital assets are homes, stocks, bonds, and cars.

Remember that in most cases, if you sell your primary residence, you can exclude the first $250k if you're single or $500k if you're married from taxes, as long as you've owned your home for two years. You do not have to report the sale to the IRS. You cannot deduct a capital loss on your primary residence, but you still have to report it.

First, you complete form 8949. If you sold multiple assets you may need to complete multiple copies of 8949. You then report that on Schedule D and on line 13 of your 1040.

You can use your capital losses to reduce your income up to $3k a year. You can carry over unused losses for use in future years.

Real estate income

All real estate income needs to be reported, even if deductions are greater than the income.

If you're claiming depreciation or car expenses, you'll need to file form 4562. You'll need to file Schedule C or Schedule E.

Real estate losses are handled several different ways, depending on the circumstances. Generally, if you own and actively manage an investment property, you can deduct up to $25k of losses against your ordinary income.

Real estate is typically considered unearned income. However, if you actively manage your property, up to 30% of net rental income can be considered earned income. If you're a real estate professional and spend an average of 20 hours a week managing your real estate business, it can all be considered earned income. Be sure to check Publication 527 for your specific situation.

Retirement income

Canadian Pension Plan (CPP) and Old Age Security (OAS) income is not taxable and doesn't have to be reported.

Registered retirement income fund (RRIF) income and withdrawals from your RRSP do need to be reported. Convert the amount from your T4RIF or T4RSP and enter it on line 16(b) of your 1040.

Previously, the IRS did not automatically recognize RRSPs and RRIFs as being tax sheltered and required the reporting of form 8891. Lots of accountants will still tell you to do this, although this changed back in 2014 and applies retroactively.

If you have enough money, you may need to file form 8938: Statement of Specified Foreign Financial Assets.

Payments from pension plans and annuities are generally taxable, since they are usually tax-deferred amounts. Check with your individual plan to make sure you're reporting the correct amounts. You need to report all retirement income on line 16b. If all of your pension and annuity income is taxable, you can leave 16a blank. If not, you'll need to report all non-taxable pension and annuity income.

A US citizen living in Canada has the first 15% of their retirement income taxed in the US and Canada can tax the rest. You can claim a foreign tax credit for the 15% taxed in the US.

Unemployment benefits

Payments for unemployment insurance, illness, and disability benefits are taxable in the US. As this is not considered earned income, this cannot be covered by the FEIE.

Social Security benefits

If you're a Canadian resident, you do not have to pay taxes on your social security income (SSI). Report your benefits on line 20a and leave 20b blank, since no portion of your benefits is taxable.

Other income

Use form 2555 or 2555-EZ to calculate your foreign earned income exclusion (FEIE). You enter this as a negative number on line 21 on your 1040.

This is also where you report gambling income, lottery winnings, and cancelled debts.

You don't have to report child support, life insurance payments, bequests, gifts, damages for injuries, veteran's benefits, welfare benefits, or workers compensation payments.

Common deductions

Most US tax deductions are included in your Schedule A.

Taxes paid can be deducted from your US income taxes. This includes Canadian federal and provincial taxes and property taxes as well as any other taxes you pay around the world, including the US.

If you claim the FEIE, you cannot deduct foreign taxes based on that income (the first $105.9k you earn). If you have foreign income over the FEIE maximum, you can determine what percentage of the income taxes you paid were for your US taxable income and deduct that amount.

If you deduct your foreign income taxes, you cannot also take the foreign tax credit. Because the deduction reduces your taxable income while the foreign tax credit reduces your taxes dollar for dollar, the foreign tax credit is often more advantageous.

Property taxes can be deducted here without interfering with your FEIE or your foreign tax credits. There is now a $10k cap on state/provincial and municipal property tax deductions, known as SALT. Any deductions you make for property taxes on a home office are in addition to this cap. You can only deduct foreign property taxes on your primary residence, not a vacation or part-time home.

You can deduct the mortgage interest for your primary residence in Canada from your US taxes. In the US, banks will give mortgage holders a form 1098, outlining the interest paid. For your Canadian mortgage, they may be willing to issue a 1098 or they can simply provide you with the necessary information.

Moving expenses are no longer deductible unless you're active duty military moving on orders.

Charitable contributions made to qualifying institutions in the US or Canada are eligible to be deducted.

Generally, foreign medications are not a deductible medical expense. Medications that you purchase and consume abroad are allowed.

Tuition and student loan interest cannot be deducted. The American Opportunity Credit and the Lifetime Learning Credit still provide tax credits for students of qualified institutions. Check the Federal Student Aid website to see if your Canadian institution qualifies. It likely does.

Owing taxes

You can only contribute to an IRA or Roth-IRA if you have income that's taxable in the US. Any income over the FEIE can be contributed to a traditional IRA up to the annual contribution limit, reducing the amount you owe in taxes. If either you or your spouse have earned income, you can contribute. You can't contribute to an IRA if you only have passive income.

If you make enough gross income or passive income in order to owe over $1k a year in taxes to the US, you may need to pay a quarterly estimated tax.

Foreign tax credits

Most Americans living in Canada who find themselves owing taxes at the end of the year are able to use foreign tax credits (FTC) to reduce or eliminate the amount owed.

You have two options for how to handle your foreign taxes paid: take the FTC or deduct the foreign taxes. If you take the FTC, you can still claim the standard deduction or itemized deductions (just don't include your Canadian income taxes).

The FTC will be complicated if you have US-based income.

Any taxes you pay in the US are recognized dollar for dollar by Canada and vice versa. This is intended to save you from double taxation.

You get two types of tax credits: earned and passive income.

You can use foreign tax credits the year you earn them, the prior year (to refile), or up to 10 years into the future. The IRS limits how many foreign tax credits you can use each year, based on the ratio of your US to world income.

Eligible taxes include Canadian federal and provincial taxes on non-US income. Property taxes and sales taxes (GST, HST, VAT) are not eligible. If you got a Canadian tax refund, you cannot include the refunded amount.

You'll need to sort your income into US and non-US income. For your non-US income, you'll need to determine if your income is passive or active and if it's covered by the Canada-US tax treaty. You'll need to complete a form 1116 for each category of income.

For each form 1116 you complete, you can also include any related deductions and losses. You can't include deductions or losses from income included in the FEIE.

In order to determine the foreign taxes paid for each category, you can divide the Canadian taxes you paid by the percentage of each type of income.

Form 1116 will also calculate the limit to the amount of FTC you can use this year. You can carry FTC back one year and forward 10 years.

Tax refunds

Some tax credits are refundable, meaning if your tax burden is zero the IRS will send you a cheque for the amount of the refundable tax credits. Non-refundable tax credits can simply bring your tax burden to zero.

If you are owed a tax refund, the easiest way to get it is direct deposit. Do not list a Canadian bank account, including a USD Canadian account. You need to provide a US bank account to get a direct deposit from the IRS.

If you don't provide direct deposit information, the IRS will mail a paper cheque to the address on your return. If you move before you get your refund, file form 8822: Change of Address.

One perk of registering with the State Department's Office of American Citizens Services is that if your refund cheque can't be delivered they can contact you.

RRSPs

Prior to October 2014, if you had an RRSP, had to file form 8891 in order to maintain their tax-deferred status in the US. This is no longer a requirement. Your RRSP is automatically recognized to have the same tax benefits as an IRA or 401k. You can deduct your RRSP contributions as if they were IRA or 401k contributions.

TFSA, RESP & RDSPs

Tax free savings accounts (TFSA), registered education savings plans (RESP), and registered disability savings plans (RDSP) were not included in the tax treaty and are not sheltered from US taxes like they're sheltered by Canadian taxes. You'll have to report and pay taxes on any income in these accounts.

The IRS does not make it clear how these accounts should be treated. Some accountants view them as trusts and suggest filing form 3520 and 3520A. Other tax experts believe they're not trusts and the 3520 and 3520A are not necessary.

It seems sufficient to report it as you would any investment income. The IRS has not made a statement to clarify the matter, much to the consternation of tax specialists and Americans living in Canada.

Given the well-documented lack of clarity regarding TFSA, RESP and RDSP, it's likely the IRS would not impose penalties for improper reporting, so long as you're reporting the income. Because your Canadian bank will likely not provide you with tax reporting information for these accounts, you will have to specifically request it or calculate it based on your financial statements.

You may find that these accounts are still beneficial for your specific tax situation. If you have tax credits, they can be used to offset any taxes you might otherwise owe in the US for investments in accounts that are tax-free in Canada. Taxes you pay on these accounts are no different than the taxes you'd pay on any other investment, they're simply not tax-free in the US like they are in Canada.

If you have a non-US spouse (both in terms of citizenship and tax treatment election) you may wish for them to hold any TFSA, RESP, and RDSPs.

Canadian mutual funds

Nearly all Canadian mutual funds and Canadian-traded ETFs are considered passive foreign investment companies (PFIC) by the IRS. If you own shares in a PFIC you need to file form 8621. If you hold these PFICs in an RRSP, you don't have to worry about this.

As a US citizen, you should probably avoid owning Canadian mutual funds outside of an RRSP, as the tax requirements are unfavorable and the reporting requirements are tedious.

Other tax-treaty items

The IRS has a lot of forms, but there isn't a form for every possible situation covered by the Canada-US tax treaty. This is what form 8833 is for.

If you aren't sure how to report income or if income needs to be reported, you can include it in form 8833 and/or a letter explaining the situation with your tax return. Of course, you should research the topic thoroughly yourself and speak to a tax professional before you do this. The IRS is not going to humor questions it finds routine, but many expats face novel tax situations where answers may not be available.

FBAR

If you have any accounts, including signing authority, at any bank outside of the US with an account value of $10k or more, you need to file a FBAR. This is true even if your income is low enough that you're not required to file US taxes.

FBAR is designed to prevent tax evasion through the use of offshore accounts.

The $10k value is for all of the accounts at the highest point in the year, so don't think you can have six $9k accounts. People make a fuss about this, but it takes five minutes (or less) and can be done online.

You need to file the FBAR online.

There is a $10k penalty for failing to file and they can assess other penalties or even pursue criminal prosecution. Are they going to do this for someone who isn't rich and committing willful tax evasion? Probably not. Do you want to find out the hard way? Nope.

For each of accounts, you'll need to provide:
- the banks' name and address,
- type of account,
- the bank account number, and
- the highest balance during the year, in US dollars.

If you have signing authority over a large number of accounts, perhaps because you're a broker, attorney, or on a number of boards, you might be in an interesting spot. The US requires that you report the accounts, but Canadian privacy law forbids doing so. In this case, you can write a letter to the IRS explaining the situation and asking for guidance.

FATCA

People love to complain about the Foreign Account Tax Compliance Act (FATCA). Accountants will pull this out to scare you into hiring them. Unless you're currently committing tax evasion by using offshore accounts, you have nothing to worry about.

FATCA is mostly a hassle for foreign financial institutions. When you open a bank account in Canada they'll ask if you're a US citizen or green card holder. You tell the truth and that's probably enough to keep you in compliance.

You might have to file form 8938: Statement of Foreign Financial Assets if you have a total of $200k USD in specified foreign assets at the end of the year or $300k USD at any point during the year. These figures are per person, so double that if you're married.

The threshold drops down to $50k and $75k if you're living in the US, so if you move back to the US and keep your accounts in Canada, don't forget to report them.

You don't need to report:
- Foreign real estate
- US mutual funds that hold foreign stocks or securities
- Art, antiques, jewelry, cars or other collectibles
- Money you have in literal cash like Scrooge McDuck
- Gold or any other precious metal

You do need to report:
- Savings, deposit, checking, and brokerage accounts
- Stocks, bonds, or interests you have in paper outside of an account
- A foreign estate, pension, or deferred compensation plan if the value your portion puts you over the threshold

If you don't know the value of your interest in a foreign pension or deferred compensation plan, the value is the value of your distributions that year. If you received no distributions, the value is zero.

If you already filed your taxes and you left out form 8938, you need to amend your return and submit it.

IRS audits

Generally, the IRS has three years in which they can audit your return. If the IRS can show that you omitted more than 25% of your income from your filing, they have six years to audit you. They also get six years if you've left off more than $5k of foreign income or failed to file a FBAR.

The IRS checks your returns against what banks and employers have filed. They also use algorithms to determine the likelihood that your return contains errors or unreported income. It's common for returns to be audited because they're incomplete or contain mathematical errors.

Things that make you more likely to be audited include: filing a schedule C, claiming a home office deduction, filing separately if you are married, and using rounded numbers rather than exact amounts. People claiming the earned income tax credit (EITC) are much more likely to be audited, as are people with a large change in income amounts not supported by W-2s or 1099s. You may also be selected for an audit if your spouse or business partner had an issue with their return.

The IRS isn't unreasonable. If you make mistakes in your tax filings and you're audited, you generally won't be penalized for it. You'll simply be required to correct them. If you realize you made a mistake and you weren't audited, you can amend tax returns from prior years.

I was audited in my early 20s. Looking back, it's obvious that I filed incorrectly. I was traveling at the time and my mom decided to simply ignore the letters they sent me (she did tell me about a wedding invitation that arrived, though). The IRS reviewed my paperwork and determined that I had overpaid by a small amount and sent me a refund. An audit doesn't necessarily mean you'll have IRS agents swarming through your house looking for receipts or whatever other nightmare scenario people imagine.

The IRS is understanding when taxpayers make honest mistakes, but they really don't like tax evasion.

How IRS audits work

There are three types of audit: a correspondence audit, an office audit, and a field audit. A correspondence audit is by far the most common, in which the IRS requests documentation for specific items.

In an office audit, you'll be required to visit an IRS office to meet with an auditor. They'll tell you what documents you need to provide ahead of time.

With a field audit, an IRS auditor will actually come to your home or business. This is very rare and reserved for high earners.

If you're audited, you want to be honest, but you also want to be careful about what information you provide. It's like talking to passport control at the airport: you want to give them information that's accurate without being unnecessarily confusing. They don't want to know your life story, they are trying to determine if you're following the rules or not. This is a multiple choice test, not an essay.

If you provide information from tax years not initially covered in the audit or say something that suggests there may be errors in other years returns, they can expand the scope of the audit.

Having all of your documents as organized as possible will help things go smoothly. This is a lot easier if your receipts are digital. It's normal for people to keep incomplete records or to make mistakes, so don't worry if your records aren't perfect.

Demonstrating that you followed IRS rules, even if you don't have all of the documents they would like to see, is called substantial compliance.

The IRS is notorious for losing documents. If they request a document, provide them with a copy and keep the original for your records.

At the end of the audit, you'll get form 4549: Proposed Changes to Tax Liability with the report and any changes to what you owe (or are owed). If you agree with the findings, you sign form 870: Consent to Proposed Tax Adjustment.

If you disagree with the findings of the audit, you can talk to the auditor, speak with their manager, appeal with the IRS, and go to court.

You have 60 days to file an appeal or the IRS findings become final.

Appendix

Canadian and US tax forms

Conveniently, most tax forms between the US and Canada have a direct equivalent. Here's how they break down.

	US	Canada
Wages	W2	T4
Other income	1099	T4A
Retirement income RESP income TFSA income	1099-R	T4A
Unemployment income	1099-G	T4E
Trust income	1099-DIV or 1041	T3
Interest income	1099-INT	T5
Social Security benefits	1099-SSA	T4AP
CPP/QPP/OAS	NR4, NR4OAS	T4AP, T4OAS
Personal tax return	1040	T1
Updated personal return	1040X	T1-ADJ
Capital gains/losses	Schedule D	Schedule 3
Dividends/interest	Schedule B	Schedule 4
Qualifying donations	Schedule A	Schedule 9
Partnership tax return	1065, K1	T5013

Key differences in Canadian & US federal income tax systems

	Canada	US
Unit	Individual	Family

Income

	Canada	US
Payment in kind	Taxable	Mostly exempt
Pension	Taxable, credits	Taxable
Social insurance	Taxable	Taxable, SS ½ taxable
Interest	Taxable	Taxable, except some state and municipal bonds
Capital gains	Partially taxable	Taxable
Primary residence	Unlimited exemption for years lived in, one per couple per year	Limited exemption based on years immediately prior to sale, one per couple in 2 years
Lottery winnings	Exempt	Taxable

Deductions & credits

	Canada	US
Dependents	Tax credit	Tax exemption
Mortgage interest	None	Deduction

State and municipal taxes	None	Deduction
Medical expenses	Credit	Deduction
Charitable contributions	Credit	Deduction
Social insurance contributions	Credit	None
Depreciation	Optional	Mandatory
Loss carry-over	Back 3 years Forward 7 years	Back 3 years Forward 15 years

US state tax filing

Each state has different methods of handling taxation. Check with your state to see exactly how each method of avoiding double taxation is applied specifically. This is a tool to help focus your own research.

State	Avoidance of double taxation
Alabama	FEIE and FTC under some circumstances
Alaska	No personal income tax
Arizona	FEIE, FTC, deduction of foreign taxes, honors tax treaty
Arkansas	FEIE, FTC, deduction of foreign taxes
California	Safe harbor
Colorado	FEIE, honors tax treaty
Connecticut	FEIE, safe harbor
Delaware	FEIE, deduction of foreign taxes, safe harbor, honors tax treaty
DC	FEIE, deduction of foreign taxes, honors tax treaty
Florida	No personal income tax
Georgia	FEIE, deduction of foreign taxes, honors tax treaty
Hawaii	FTC, deduction of foreign taxes in some circumstances
Idaho	FEIE, deduction of foreign taxes, safe harbor

Illinois	FEIE, honors tax treaty
Indiana	FEIE, FTC, honors tax treaty
Iowa	FTC, deduction of foreign taxes, honors tax treaty
Kansas	FEIE, FTC, deduction of foreign taxes
Kentucky	FEIE
Louisiana	FEIE, FTC with restrictions, deduction of foreign taxes
Maine	FEIE, FTC for foreign jurisdictions that share a border with a US state, safe harbor, honors tax treaty
Maryland	Foreign tax deduction ***Conflicting information regarding FEIE***
Massachusetts	FTC for Canada, honors tax treaty
Michigan	FEIE, FTC for Canadian provinces, honors tax treaty
Minnesota	FEIE, FTC for Canadian provinces, foreign tax deduction except for Canadian provinces, honors tax treaty
Mississippi	FEIE, foreign tax deduction
Missouri	FEIE, foreign tax deduction, safe harbor, honors tax treaty
Montana	FEIE, FTC with limitations, foreign tax deduction, honors tax treaty
Nebraska	FEIE, foreign tax deduction, honors tax treaty
Nevada	No personal income tax

New Hampshire	No personal income tax
New Jersey	
New Mexico	FEIE, foreign tax deduction, honors tax treaty
New York	FEIE, FTC for Canadian provinces, safe harbor, honors tax treaty
North Carolina	FEIE, FTC, honors tax treaty
North Dakota	FEIE
Ohio	FEIE, honors tax treaty
Oklahoma	FEIE, foreign tax deduction, safe harbor, honors tax treaty
Oregon	FEIE, foreign tax deduction, safe harbor, honors tax treaty
Pennsylvania	
Rhode Island	FEIE, honors tax treaty
South Carolina	FEIE, FTC for states and provinces, foreign tax deduction, honors tax treaty
South Dakota	No personal income tax
Tennessee	Only taxes personal investment income
Texas	No personal income tax
Utah	FEIE, foreign tax deduction, honors tax treaty

Vermont	FEIE, FTC for Canadian provinces, foreign tax deduction, honors tax treaty
Washington	No personal income tax
West Virginia	FEIE, safe harbor, honors tax treaty
Wisconsin	FEIE, honors tax treaty
Wyoming	No personal income tax

Canadian and US business deductions

Deductions are fairly consistent between the two countries. By keeping the differences in mind when tracking expenses, you can make it easy to adjust the numbers accordingly when it comes time to file.

Remember that the specifics of what's allowed in each category may differ between countries.

US	Canada
Capital expenses	
Depreciation	Capital cost allowance
Costs of goods and services	Costs of goods and services
Startup and organizational costs	Business start-up costs
Self-employed expenses	
Health insurance premiums	Other business expenses
Moving expenses	
Retirement plans	Salaries, wages, and benefits
Self-employment taxes	Business tax, fees, licenses, and dues
Student loan interest	

Standard business expenses

Advertising	Advertising
Bad debt	Bad debt
Bank fees	Business tax, fees, licenses, and dues
Charitable donations	
Conventions and trade shows	Other business expenses
Education	Other business expenses
Insurance	Insurance
Interest	Interest charges
Home office	Business-use-of-home
Legal, accounting, and professional fees	Legal, accounting, and professional fees Management and administration fees
Maintenance, repairs, and renovations	Maintenance and repairs
Meals and entertainment	Meals and entertainment
Non-cash gifts and rewards	
Office supplies, tools, and services	Supplies Office expenses Delivery, freight, and express

Parking fees, tolls, and local transit	Travel
Rent and property leases	Rent
Research and development	Other business expenses
Salaries and wages	Salaries, wages, and property taxes
Utilities	Telephone and utilities Fuel costs (non-vehicle)
Taxes	Business tax, fees, licenses, and dues
Travel	Travel
Software	Office expenses
Vehicle expenses	Motor vehicle expenses

Sample TFSA / RESP / RDSP letter to the IRS

Re: Canadian tax-deferred accounts

To Whom It May Concern:

I am a US tax resident living in Canada. As the holder of a [TFSA/RESP/RDSP] I have been given conflicting advice regarding the appropriate way to declare this investment income.

These types of accounts are omitted from the tax treaty between the US and Canada and the IRS has not offered guidance.

It appears that the most appropriate way to report this income is to treat it as I would any investment income paying dividends and interest. This is how I have reported it on my return for [tax year] and how I will continue to report future earnings. Please let me know if this is not correct so I can amend my return and take any other necessary actions.

I would appreciate if you could provide guidance on the appropriate way to report this income.

Sincerely,

Sample penalty abatement request letter

Re: Request for Penalty Abatement

To Whom It May Concern:

I am writing to request the abatement of penalties, to the sum of $[penalty amount] assessed according to the notice [notice date] for the tax year [tax year].

I [paid late/filed late/failed to report income] because [I was seriously ill/my home was destroyed in a fire/other reasonable cause].

Attached are documents providing further details of the circumstances that prevented me from being able to [pay/file] my tax obligations [on time/accurately]. Please find enclosed:
- [Supporting document 1]
- [Supporting document 2]
- [Supporting document 3]

Payment of the taxes owed [is attached/has been made/is proposed in the attached payment schedule form/is included for this offer of compromise], minus penalties assessed.

Please accept this petition for abatement of penalties due to reasonable cause.

Sincerely,

Be sure to include relevant supporting documents to demonstrate reasonable cause. Do not send original documents, copies are sufficient and the IRS mail lose or fail to return originals.

If you are unable to make the payment in full, include forms for an offer in compromise or a payment plan.

About the author

Cori Carl immigrated to Canada through Express Entry's Federal Skilled Worker Program in 2016. She published Moving to Canada detailing the immigration process. She writes about her immigration experience on WelcomeHomeOntario.ca.

Before moving to Toronto, she spent ten years in Brooklyn and grew up on the Jersey Shore. She is an avid traveler and history nerd who writes about her adventures in the sharing economy on Remote Swap.club.

She works as a communications consultant for mission driven organizations and serves family and professional caregivers around the world as director of The Caregiver Space.

Cori has a BA in media and cultural studies from the New School University and an MA in communications from Baruch College, both in New York City.

Old Age Security?

Pete can have a solo 401k

- gifts made 3 or less years before death we will still need to pay the deemed disposition tax (estate tax)
- when die, they calculate as if all investments were sold.

- ① Set Mom up w/ credit card
- ② Does she get a tax reduction for charitable gifts?
  ↳ better to give to charities while still alive.
- ③ transfer-on-death account?
- ④ Be sure beneficiaries are me + Andrew for all bank accounts